D1486574

I'M RUNNING AWAY FROM HOME,
BUT I'M NOT ALLOWED
TO CROSS THE STREET

I'M RUNNING AWAY FROM HOME,
BUT I'M NOT ALLOWED
TO CROSS THE STREET

A PRIMER OF WOMEN'S LIBERATION

BY

GABRIELLE BURTON

DRAWINGS BY DIANNE FOOTLICK

KNOW, INC.
PITTSBURGH

Published August 1972
Second Printing December 1972

Library of Congress Card No. 76-182740
International Standard Book No. 0-912786-00-0

KNOW, INC., Box 86031, Pittsburgh, 15221

Printed in the United States of America

This book is lovingly dedicated to:

my sisters in the "Sojourner Truth" consciousness-raising group, who never once doubted
that I could do it.

Roger, who was "educable" and consistently
offered support, encouragement, belief, and
love. Not to mention hours of typing . . .

Maria Christina, Jennifer, Ursula, and Gabri-
ella, who cheerfully endured gluts of television,
babysitters, and peanut butter sandwiches so
that "Momma" could write. And to ? in
utero*, who behaved itself throughout both
gestations–its own and this book's.

*The feminist movement was increased by one by the
arrival of Charity Heather on August 29th. Those present at her birth attest to the fact that she emerged
into the world with a lusty cry and a clenched fist.

ENLIGHTENMENT

I'M RUNNING AWAY FROM HOME . . . is a firstling. It is a "first" for the author, illustrator, typesetter, editors, proof-readers, collaters, printers, and publishers, all of whom are feminists. In the birthing and rearing processes, we did as all new parents do—we "practiced" on the first, supplementing our lack of "know-how" with generous amounts of belief, good intentions, and hope. All things considered, we are pleased with and proud of our initial progeny. We present it without apology.

FOREWORD

Betty Friedan, Kate Millett, and Germaine Greer have already written definitive books on the Women's Movement. Like the three sisters, the books are brilliant, beautiful, and have a lot of class. I keep the trilogy by my front door so that anyone who enters will know where I stand. But none of these books are ones that a person reads in her bathtub. They contain such a wealth of unfamiliar, challenging insights that even the determined reader often succumbs to the temptation to tackle them another day. This primer is to read in that interim.

During the past year, I have read copiously on the Women's Movement–devouring every available source from "prestige papers," hastily assembled anthologies, to the scraggiest underground spin-offs. Simultaneously, I became a "public speaker," shakingly facing such formidable audiences as the "Friday Evening Baptist Potluck Get-Together" and the local Kiwanis Club. I shared and compared my findings from these avenues with other women who were exploring different areas for new answers to our questions. In this book I have tried to gather all the important, elementary concepts of the Movement into a single source and present them simply–from one who remembers the brain pounding endured in my first bout with "The Big Three." Movement pioneers may find many of these ideas "old stuff," but the book remains deliberately that way. It is affectionately geared to the woman who was off scouring her sink when the *Feminine Mystique* began stirring deeper waters.

I have also tried to recapture my initial fears, prejudices, and forebodings upon joining the Movement. And most important, to tell it from one who has been there–the lady with five kids and a house so messy that the Department of Sanitation threatened to condemn it–who has to find different solutions than the teenager, single woman, or street person. My gropings will not exactly parallel anyone else's, but hopefully they will encompass enough similarities to ease a reader's struggles and provide a base from which to start her own gropings.

True to my belief that there is humor in the most moribund matter, I have tried to incorporate light touches into my rendering. This is a very precarious line to tread–the Movement has often been written about humorously, but never without distortion and condescension. I found that on occasion the thinking and the telling dredged up so many sensitive areas that my smile grew a little wan.

In the overlapping, inter-twined search for answers, often I would happen upon a catchy phrase or a well-turned concept and I would carefully tuck the small jewel away for future use.

With time, the original sources faded and I became cheerfully deluded that all these clever incisive gems emanated from my own marvelous gray matter. In going back over this primer, I have tried to credit as many of these lines or ideas as possible to their original thinker. But the mind is undependable and many of the used sources have long since disappeared. If I have plagiarized anyone's exact phrasing or clever quip, be kind, sister, and know that it was unintentional. In a real sense, this reflects the co-operative essence of the Movement itself–women working together to grope toward new ideas and expressions and then generously and eagerly sharing them with other women.

So reader, accept it as it's offered–with hope and encouragement, affection and sisterhood. It is an invitation–read it in the tub–let it pick up jelly smudges from the kitchen table. It is a book to be kept by your back door.

WHAT'S A NICE GIRL LIKE ME DOING IN A PLACE LIKE THIS?

Making Soap can be FUN!

FREE OUR SISTERS FREE OURSELVES

NOW

CHAPTER 1

WHAT'S A NICE GIRL LIKE ME
DOING IN A PLACE LIKE THIS?

To say that a lot of men are hostile to the Women's Liberation Movement is like saying that Ralph Nader doesn't like cheats. Last week, I went to a neighborhood bakery to have a cake made for a feminist friend. In the middle of it, I wanted a drawing of Olive Oil giving the clenched fist salute, surrounded by: the slogan, "POWER TO THE SISTERS!", a few scattered female biological symbols, and a balloon here and there. Just a cheerful, happy birthday cake, but the baker did not want to do it. After a long hassle, he finally agreed–but when I went to pick it up, this well-established, stolid, suburban baker had written on the side of the cake in red frosting, "NUTS!" Such is the depth of feeling being generated by the Movement.

I don't have any of this with my husband. He is the nicest guy in the world. There have been times in our marriage that I have considered this a drawback, like in dealing with department stores. "Nice Guys Finish LAST!" I have been heard to shriek. But over the long haul, he has convinced me that a calm spirit combined with a civil tongue is generally effective and a lot less tolling.

So when I decided to liberate myself, I had the ideal environment: a mate who was a calm, rational, open person. The only possible obstacle was his excess of caution. Being a scientist, his inclination was to wait–to observe–and to measure any revolutionary proposition. When I insisted that we enter the experiment, this is how the Liberation Front has gone at our house.

A local church was sponsoring a discussion of WL, led by real live liberationists. I wanted to go, ostensibly out of curiosity, secretly out of hope.

It was a spirited discussion. When we entered, several men were shouting variations of "Ahhhhh, you think you got it bad! What about me? I gotta wear a tie and work a job I hate."

The WL women were very sympathetic, saying, "Right. RIGHT! We're ALL oppressed! We've got to work TOGETHER!"

Later, my husband, Roger, said in a soft voice, "There's no doubt that women are severely discriminated against in many ways, especially in the academic fields. I really understand your . . . "

"*YOU* UNDERSTAND! *YOU* UNDERSTAND! HOW DARE you understand!" came this shriek at him. The woman was furious. She accused him of patronizing, of condescension, of male chauvinism—while I tried to say that he was a really nice guy and she misunderstood. That was Roger's first introduction to the Movement.

Several months went by while I avoided any contact with WL. Finally I decided to go to an orientation meeting. As I said, "This movement is going to be an important historical happening. It's current events. It's practically my duty to go and keep myself informed." (Never mind that I'm bleeding inside and maybe I can find some solace, some direction, some hope.)

I left the house with a small chip on my shoulder. "Just make one crack I dare you." He didn't.

I entered the meeting with trepidation. The place would probably be full of man-hating, aggressive kinds of females. (As far as the casual eye could see, I had made a splendid success of the American middle class dream. I was Julia Child, Mary Poppins, and Earth Mother rolled into one successful, fulfilled woman. Nobody knew that I screamed at Roger and the kids inside the closed door. Still, I wasn't going to trade in my charade till I knew I was getting something better.)

I certainly didn't want to get tied in with any bra-burning radicals. I never understood those pushy women who burned their bras at the Miss America pageant.* Seemed like kind of a perverted thing to do. *I* had always wanted to be Miss America. They were probably all small-chested.

One of the first things I surreptitiously checked out was how many were wearing bras. Most were. In fact, there were a lot of respectable-looking women there, soft-spoken and carefully groomed. "Funny," I thought, "What are nice looking women like that doing in a place like this?"

There was a visual presentation of the Movement's aims and after, we formed into groups to talk. Ours opted to continue on a weekly basis. I volunteered my house for the first meeting. ("For crying out loud, it's half my house too. What's a house for if not to have your friends in? What in God's name will I do with Roger?")

I came home from that first meeting, bursting with vague glimpses into a brave new world. Roger gave me a little scientific speech

---

*The infamous Miss America bra-burning never took place. Such action was intended as a symbolic protest against the literal and figurative restriction of women–but red tape foiled the plan when a fire permit was denied. Feminist pyromania is merely a fantasy kindled by the media.

on the risk of tampering with well-established sex roles. I really flipped. Here I'm seeing a little light at the end of the morass and he's talking about cross-cultural research. Paraphrasing the angry woman liberationist of a few months before, I say, "How could you *possibly* understand my suffering?" and slam to bed.

Excitement overtakes my quick temper and I keep sharing the new insights I'm gleaning. When he brings up research to challenge something, I question his sincerity, "Do you really want me to be happy or not, Roger?"

He did and I knew it. We had ridden eight years of marriage at various emotional peaks and depths, during which I had produced four daughters, got involved in the community, took up tennis and skiing–in general, became a well-rounded woman. Every time I had another baby, I would feel creative and fulfilled–for a while. Then that sinking feeling would come that there was another five years until I could get out. "Get out from what?" Roger would puzzle. "From under," was my opaque reply. He couldn't understand what it was all about. Good reason for that. *I* couldn't understand what it was all about. My life was exactly as I had been taught it should be.

I had always planned on marriage and maternity. ("What do you want to be when you grow up, little girl?" "A mother.") I went to parochial schools for sixteen years and was willing putty, eager to be molded into a "real" woman. I learned what my "particular" gifts were and what my needs were. Then I went out searching for half a man who needed to be inspired, consoled, and nourished.

I never made any bones about it. I couldn't understand why some of my peers were devious, practicing their snares in secret. Marriage was my vocation, my *career*. Being attractive and bright, I soon found my "other half" and he gave me the golden American dream.

He was a professional, so *I* had great status–we had a beautiful baby–we bought the house in the coveted suburb–we luxuriated. I was able to add layers to this basic essence in the ensuing years–more children, an addition to the house, professional honors for my husband–but I had the crux of the thing at age 24. This used to give me an uncomfortable feeling but you don't go around flagellating yourself because you got rich too soon.

You also don't go around complaining when your husband has already given you everything, unless you feel very secure in your relationship or are very unhappy. I was both.

We would have periods of deep satisfaction, contentment, fun. Then out of the blue, a grievance would emerge. I would attack a specific aspect of our life and pin everything on it. My Rage Of The

Month might be directed toward our house—I might lash out against the neighborhood. Sometimes it was housework. The boredom. I tried them all. We would then try to relieve the specific problem but the unease never went away.

I attributed these imbalances to various things. They were probably post-partum, pre-partum, or intra-partum depressions. The pill took responsibility for a while. I didn't like to think about it too much because I was afraid that there was something wrong with *me*—some basic lack that kept me from being truly fulfilled.

I threw myself into my "career." I was determined to erase the vague unease by making myself more of a woman. I already was interested in natural childbirth and breastfeeding. I never even wore slacks, preferring skirts for the soft, rounded womanly image. But obviously I had been over-educated in some areas and ill-equipped in others. I had learned all the philosophy of housewifery but had never been taught the specifics, like cleaning toilets.

I read books on how to increase my efficiency. They had fascinating chapters, like "Making Your Own Soap Can Be Fun," and inspirational ones, like "You Can TOO Breastfeed Quadruplets." I marveled at these superhuman earthmothers who were saving their runned nylons and doing creative things with aluminum foil. I tried many of their suggestions, but my heart wasn't in it.

During this time, I read *The Feminine Mystique*, but that was a second-caste book. Everyone knew Betty Friedan was divorced. Ahah! Bitter, with axes to grind. She had failed in the dream so everything she said was suspect. Never mind that I agreed with it all.

As an antidote, I read Phyllis McGinley on the joys of housewifery. That was a beautiful book and put old Freidan right in her place. I polished silver and bubbled three-day soups and oh! the splendor of it all! But in the back of my brain, Miss McGinley's Pulitzer prize and live-in help kept getting in the way.

I read most of the time–in between sleeping. I wasn't working. I had stopped that when we were married, knowing it would undermine my husband's role as the PROVIDER. I lay around for nine months and ten days, waiting for my first fulfillment to come. I insisted that I loved being a housewife. Roger suggested once, in between my sobbings, that maybe I'd be happier if I went out and did something. What did he know? *I* knew with my extraordinary sensitivity that his ego would be shattered if I brought in a buck. Besides it would all fall into place when the baby was born.

I slept inordinate amounts. It made me very guilty, but it also made the day go away and that was more important.

Daytime sleeping is a form of suicide. Amazing numbers of women resort to it. Everybody knows it and pretends it is a necessity when raising small children. When a woman telephones another in the afternoon, she often says, "I hope I didn't wake you." It is common to hear, "Don't call between one and three. That's my naptime."

This waste of human potential is incalculable. The psychological damage it does to a woman's self-concept is infinitely more so. Daytime is the time for adults to be up. People with responsible jobs, people who have anything important, valued, or interesting to do don't sleep in the middle of the afternoon.

Afternoon naptime is part of the sacred time that mothers spend with their children. It's a together kind of thing to do, lying side by side for a couple of hours. There are those terrible times when the children don't want to sleep, having something more interesting to do. Poor momma is frantic because she needs it so much. She holds them down–it's for their own good.

I asked a doctor once for some pep pills to keep me awake long enough so that I could change my pattern of afternoon naps. He said, "Little children are very fatiguing. You'd be surprised how many young mothers sleep in the afternoon."

"I wouldn't be at all," I replied, "But if I taught school or ran an orphanage, I wouldn't find it necessary to take a three-hour break in the middle of the afternoon." He laughed (kindly) and said (paternally), "Now don't you worry about it. You're normal." I *knew* I was normal. My whole block was snoring. I just wanted to be vertical.

Some women use up their days by taking adult education courses. This is an improvement over sleeping. I tried this route too. French. Speedreading. Anthropology. Ceramics. I liked them all. There was very little difference between me and my children. Me rushing to my dancing class while they rushed to their dancing class.

Middle class women often ask, "What are you taking this year?" It is viewed as a satisfactory adjustment, not as a group of creative humans frittering away their talents and energies like pampered, lavished children. How many men take adult education courses with never a specific goal in mind other than to keep interested and interesting.

Some women invest in perpetual consuming. I did this. Spending money was a sphere in which I had some power–the scope to make decisions. Figuring out unit prices keeps brain cells from complete atrophy. I took lengthy times to decide between piecrusts and detergents. I pored over the bargains, buying September school clothes on January sales. I was making a real contribution to my family's welfare by being an intelligent consumer. I was also making a lot of time go away.

I passed eight years in these ways.

My friends all considered me a great success–the most relaxed mother on the block. Few people knew of my discontent. It was not something I could articulate well, and I was ashamed that I felt it. I had no consistent culprits to accuse, no constructive alternatives to propose. There was only the recurring thought, "There's got to be more than this."

I finally sought out the Women's Liberation Movement because of my constant guilt over daytime sleeping. Every afternoon, I would think, "I am going to wake up and discover that I am old and have never done anything with my life except sleep away time." Then I would lie down and take my nap.

I went there with nothing to lose. It was a last ditch attempt with no high expectations. Perhaps I might be able to save my daughters. I knew that my life was irrevocably beyond my control.

They told me I still had a chance. All around me there were women who had experienced the same things I had felt so guilty about. It wasn't me. It was something outside of me, and we were going to change it. The time had come in time for me.

Roger is right to take my enthusiasm with a grain of salt. He has seen panaceas come and go. But it doesn't matter. This is it, and I still have a chance.

SISTERHOOD IS POWERFUL

CHAPTER 2

SISTERHOOD IS POWERFUL

R. "What do you talk about in your group week after week?"
G. "Just stuff."

Friendship is considered one of the deep pleasures of life, but most of us make do without it. We fill up the gaps with numerous social contacts, sucking emotional scraps from each one. In our culture we do not encourage friendship. It interferes with competition. You can't reach the moon–raise the GNP–run a society on friendship. It is not efficient.

When I was nine, I had friends. I joined a gang, and for three years it provided camaraderie, support, stimulation, and affection on a regular basis. I gave it up readily for popularity.

My goals shifted. At twelve, I was more interested in being admired and desired than having friends. I kept just one friendship from that early gang; throughout my teens, she was the only girl I ever related to as a *person*.

Other girls were competitors or co-conspirators. If they were closer to my goals than I was, I strove to be like them. I took bits from most girls I met, a walk from this one, style of clothes from that one, a mysterious look from another; but, except for the one friend, I never related to any of them as unique human beings, valuable and interesting in their own right.

Most of us weren't interesting in our own right. We thought of ourselves as objects, and we measured our worth by our relation to the subjects, i.e., boys. Even then we wore other people's status easily and eagerly. If you went with the captain of the football team, *you* were successful. All young people are unformed. We were no more amorphous than most, but we were not searching for shapes. We were searching for partners who had shapes.

Around age 15, my goals again shifted slightly. I continued to want and enjoy the admiration that popularity brings, but I missed the pleasures of friendship. I sought my friends among the *boys*. They were the interesting people in my sphere–the dynamic ones. One could talk ideas with boys; one talked only about people with girls. Already I had absorbed the bias that girls are passive and inherently limited. Small wonder I wanted to be "one of the boys." But the boys didn't want me to be one of them. Gonads were always breaking up beautiful friendships. Against all evidence, I kept believing it was possible and right to have boy-*friends*.

At age 22, I was still trying to maintain a close asexual relationship with a man. He was fun and interesting; I was fun and interesting; obviously a fun, interesting friendship was in store. He told me bluntly that he could waste no more time on such a dead-end relationship. Either it was going to be fruitful sexually or as potential wifely material, but he had neither time nor need for girl-*friends*. I accepted his explanation as valid and terminated the relationship. My female conditioning was so thorough that ten years passed before I realized that what he really said was that I was good as a body or as a property, but not as a person.

I married soon after and we moved away. The wives of my husband's friends became my "friends." They were easy, smiling relationships; we had spouses' careers and mutual acquaintances in common. One never imposed depressions, fears, or tears on them.

I was not close to my neighbors. I live in a neighborhood which prides itself on the maintenance of privacy. One is always there to help out in a major emergency; but in the minor ones, like loss of sanity or identity, we never interfere. After the birth of our second child, Roger shouted the news to our next-door neighbor. The neighbor congratulated him in great surprise; she hadn't known I was pregnant! Our houses are twelve feet apart. Of course, she had her own problems and drank her days away, but I never interfered with her privacy.

When we first moved in, I sat in our brand new house, holding a shiny newborn, waiting for someone to come and say, "Welcome to this street! To this community! To this way of life!" I waited there for an entire summer with the doors open and a dying grin on my mouth, waiting for acknowledgement. No one ever came. They didn't want to disturb me. So much for neighbors. *

Then there were parties. I met two kinds of women at parties, the professionals and the housewives. The housewives were dull and spoke of dull things. While the men discussed important issues, they swapped chicken soup recipes. Such things are a good and valid part of life, but a steady diet of recipes leaves the soul hungry.

While the toilet-training women bored me, I bored the professionals. I had no credentials. I felt so inferior to them that I was blank in their presence. They were always asking, "What do you

*My neighborhood is changing. Apparently, many people are beginning to desire increased community.

do?'' I did what a woman was supposed to do: I raised children and kept a house and they showed me what society really thinks of that. "But what do you *do*?'' they would persist. Finally I would be forced to say it out loud, "I'm just a housewife.'' I hated them.

Let's hear it for friends and neighbors! Once you got past the pretty bromides, one learned another bizarre fact of modern life: Most people go through their entire lives without friends and without community. I thought it unfortunate, but then many things are unfortunate, like war and pollution and hunger. Tuck it away in another "Tsk! Tsk! Wouldn't it be nice if . . .?'' category.

I certainly wasn't in the market for women friends. I personally enjoyed being a woman, but only because I had escaped many of the dreadful traits inflicted on women by nature. My bias against women had increased over the years. It wasn't the hysteria or the clucking or the petti-ness that bothered me: I opted out on the DULLNESS. Women just weren't interesting. Occasionally one might surmount her nature and *do* something, but that kind generally became too much like men.

When I volunteered my house for the first meeting of the Women's Liberation discussion group, it was not because of the women; it was in spite of them. That Women's Liberation was made up of women seemed to be one of those trying things one had to work with. No doubt it would make a herculean task more difficult. God knows how women can never make up their minds. Agree on anything. Get organized. Stop giggling.

Twenty women came to that first meeting.* It was an intensely stimulating, enjoyable evening. The hours flew as we began to discover ourselves—to grope toward common bonds. I had hoped it would be beneficial; I had never dreamed that it would be enjoyable. That night, I took my first small step toward switching my identity and allegiance to women.

From that first twenty, twelve remained permanent. This is The Group: the women in it are dynamic, exciting people. They are not unique; they are not exceptions. Perhaps some of them were those same housewives and professionals I once felt so apart from. I see and hear them differently now. They *are* different now. They have revealed themselves and in so doing, have proven all my anti-woman prejudices wrong.

---

*Roger didn't disgrace me by eavesdropping or coming out and protesting his innocence, "Why, some of my best friends are women. Let me get you a cup of coffee. See, I'm not an oppressor . . ." He stayed upstairs and acted as if the whole meeting were of most common nature.

I was wrong to blame women for all those tedious parties of years past. Look more closely at current social scenes with mixed groups. When women huddle in their "toilet-training" corners, it is not because of any intrinsic dullness; it is because they are seldom allowed out of them. When a woman tries to break down her invisibility and offer her thoughts to a group of men, she is accorded her moment. Gentlemanly attention is given her. Afterwards, it's as if someone belched or farted–politely, her interruption is ignored. The men's conversation resumes, with the woman slowly, excruciatingly ignored. Most women do not have the temerity or the confidence to persist. It only takes a few rebuffs before they retreat gratefully to their corners where they are acknowledged as contributing human beings with some worth.

Much of it is tied up with proper credentials. Child-rearing and managing a house are the only credentials many women are allowed to assume. ("Ask my wife. She runs the house. I don't know a thing about it. She's the expert.") Politics. war, "important" issues are left to the men.

Sometimes men experience this exclusion also. The only lawyer in a group of medical doctors can be frozen out of the conversation. But most men, by sheer aggressiveness, can force the conversations to include them. Women are not used to being overtly aggressive. They withdraw, thus perpetuating the myth that women don't really have interest or knowledge in other areas anyway. It is a self-fulfilling prophecy. Though it is HOG-WASH, I bought it for many years, and so did a mass of other women.

ALL of the women I have met through the Movement are stimulating, bright, creative, interesting human beings. If women are dull, docile, simpering it is only because they have been forced to be that way. They have accepted the stereotype in order to survive–to pass.

Now when I go to parties, I seek out the women. I want to find out what they're *really* thinking, feeling, doing. I identify with them. I have learned to respect them and in the process to respect myself. I get my recipes out of the newspaper food section these days. Nobody is swapping them at parties anymore. We are too busy becoming friends. We are also learning to relate to each other in non-competitive ways. ("Am I the prettiest one here? The second prettiest? The third?") I've been to some great parties lately.

At our weekly group meeting we talk to one another. Sometimes we cry in front of one another. We laugh too. And touch. It is the only group of people I know in which it is possible to show all of one's human dimensions. (It is permissible to go into most gatherings only if one is in a good mood–smiling–has something to contribute. A guest has a certain duty, you know. Don't forget to say, "Thank you." Stay home if you've only got glum. We've got enough glum of our own.) We meet once a week at each other's houses. We never miss. It is a firm commitment and a pleasurable one.

It was not always so pleasurable. We had to work at it. The first weeks were rambling and tedious. I would sit there thinking, "My God, it's like the rest. Nobody's *really* talking. It's a waste of time." One or two useful thoughts generally emerged during an evening, and on the strength of those, I would go back. I had no alternative. The other social groups I was in weren't even trying to talk.

Weeks turned into months before the gabble focused, the barriers lowered, and the fears dissolved. We developed.*

---

*Many city-dwellers don't have the opportunity or the inclination to *develop* relationships. We are busy, fast-paced, and transient. We make quick decisions and are unused to waiting for the latent parts of things to bloom.

Big city social intercourse is often a constant round of meeting people and introducing them to other people. People may have only one occasion to prove their worth. You can turn off, or be turned off, by one statement. ("You blew it, baby, I thought you were nice, but I see from *that* remark that you are hopeless–neo-fascist–uncool–perverted. I was going to ask you to dinner, and I had these really interesting people I wanted you to meet. But now...")

Simultaneously, while dealing a death blow to potential relationships, many of us mourn the shallowness of our present ones. If we really want meaningful relationships, we have to invest in them–to be patient while they ripen. We have to stop having our expectations

In our group, we speak intimately of our personal experiences. We are disparate in age and background, but this is transcended by the similar experiences we have shared because of gender. Both the professional woman and the housewife must deal with the problems of running the house, raising the children, and trying to *be* someone. Both must cope with the humilitating images of woman perpetuated by the media. The professional woman competing in a "man's world" has to struggle constantly to prove she is still "feminine"– a "real" woman. The housewife has to show she is not *just* a "feminine" woman but has some interests outside her mundane sphere. They are reverse sides of one coin with the woman manipulated on either side into having to *prove* her value, by conforming to someone else's definition.

At our weekly discussions, we piece together these common parts of our experiences to recognize prevailing conditions that stifle us all. We carefully look at society so we can see what it's done to us and what we can do about it.

From recognition, we can go on to change society–to effect our personal reality as each of

either fulfilled or dashed in a five minute trial period. ("Vibrations" have a romantic appeal but they are often wrong. Perhaps antennae become dulled from constant decisions, rather than sharpened.)

us sees it. This is necessarily both an individual and a collective process. It is individual because there is no one destiny for all women. My choices will be different from Barbara's, Sadie's, or Faith's because *I* am different. We each have our unique wants, needs, and aspirations. In the past, spouses, priests, economists, and sociologists told us what we were and what we should be. Now each of us is making that decision.

However, one quickly realizes that there are no personal "solutions" possible. This is because it is not a personal "problem." Initially, most women join a group because of their personal unhappiness without realizing the ramifications of that unhappiness. A group can help individuals find partial alternatives, but eventually it must function as a collective action to change basic social structures. A woman can rearrange individual things that hold her back–she can have her husband share the housework and child-care–but her arrangements do her little good if they only free her to experience job discrimination.

Massive social change must occur: establishment of daycare centers, equal pay for equal work, re-education of children, etc. Thus the personal group becomes of necessity a political action. This is what is meant by the current maxim: The personal is political.

In the group we use a specialized way to talk to one another, called raising consciousness.

This technique increases our sensitivity to the various forms of oppression in our lives. In order to adjust successfully to our conditions, most of us have had to develop elaborate blinders. Raising consciousness helps us recognize our blinders and let out our angers and frustrations so that we can take hold of our lives and rechannel ourselves. Ideally one raises consciousness to the point where one can and must change her life.

Anger must be recognized before it is possible to exorcise it. If it is not in focus, it spills over into unrelated things and never gets resolved. When I used to rage about the house, the boredom, or the housework, I was never able to "solve my problem" because the focus was wrong. I was blaming symptoms, not causes.

Raising consciousness is done in different ways. Some groups do it in a structured fashion, with a specific topic for each meeting, such as "How do you feel about your mother?" or "Were there differences in how you and your brothers were raised?" Other groups are free-form flow of consciousness, letting come out what does. Generally, our group uses this latter approach. It is successful because we are very compatible and share many similar wave lengths. We utilize the more structured approach when we feel we are growing too tangential. Either approach is very personal. It is not possible to challenge private parts of one's

life-style and beliefs–to speak of shattered illusions–
and remain objective and uninvolved.

In the beginning, it was scary to reveal
ourselves. We were all hindered by the fear that
our unhappiness was our personal failure–the old
sore that eats at women about whether we're
real women or not. We felt guilty speaking of
ourselves. What *right* did we have to take care of
our own lives when there were so many others to
take care of? ("Woman is a Giver.") When
Chinese guerillas raise consciousness, they are
revolutionary; when women do it, we are selfish.

Our fears were real, but they were unfounded.
We chanced censure or rejection and neither came;
guilt went home early.

Consciousness-raising is not necessarily pain-
ful or intense. Sometimes it is merely a bringing
to one's awareness the subtle implications of a
common term, as in the following:

N. in telling a story, says, "Then the girls said . . ."

"Excuse me, N.," cuts in G., "but I'm really beginning to take exception to your using 'girls' when
you're speaking about women."

N. is perplexed. "Whatever for? I always use
it. I like it."

G.: "Well, let's kick it around a little. What does
'girls' mean to you?"

S.: "Girls are frivolous–girls are cute–girls are
young . . ."

B.: "No, they're not. My mother is 64 and she and the 'girls' still get together every week to play bridge."

D.: "Sure, and the 'boys' go out for a night of bowling."

G.: "That's just it. When the 'boys' go out, it implies a night *out*–a kicking over of the traces–an irresponsibility. Just think about it. 'Boys will be boys.' The 'boys' are going to play poker. The 'boys' are bowling. Always a time *off*. Can you imagine the head of General Motors saying to his top executives, 'What do you boys think we ought to do about Ralph Nader?' or President Nixon saying, 'I'm going to get together with some of the boys in the Cabinet.' "

D.: "But generals talk about 'our boys' in the services."

S.: "Yes, but that's a very paternal use. Men in the army are 'boys' in the sense that they have no control over their lives. Decisions are made where to move them, what they'll do, etc. *That's* one of the things I object to in the term 'girls.' The inherent paternalism. 'Well what are you girls up to now?' "

G.: "I think one big reason we readily call ourselves 'girls' is the youth cult in our country. Everybody wants to stay young forever. 'Girls' are young and delightful and irresponsible.

'Women' sounds deadly. We don't have any of the European tradition of women becoming more attractive as they mature. Like Melina Mercouri. She's 46, and look how fantastic she is. Or Anouk Aimee. Our 40 year olds are Doris Day and Debbie Reynolds, and they get younger every day. Or we have young stars (in their 30's) like Ali McGraw, who specialize in playing 'girls.' To think of picking some unformed adolescent, no matter how charming, over a *woman*, would be laughable to a European. I must say, as I get older and older, this seems like a much more civilized way to do things." (Laughter.)

F.: "I want to get back to 'boys' implying irresponsibility and think of that in terms of 'girls.' I object to 'girls'–I think it subtly undermines our self-concept when we see ourselves as 'girls.' Some of us go from being 'Daddy's girl' to our husband's 'best girl.' At what point do we stand up and become mature, responsible, adult women?"

S.: "I was just playing *Carousel* for my kids and I always loved the Soliloquy he sings when he discovers he's going to be a father. Well, I just realized what a sexist song that is. It really stereotypes. Like it goes, 'My little girl, pink and white, bashful as girls should be. My little girl gets hungry every night, and she comes home to me.' When he sings about a son, the boy is strong and independent, etc. It really bugged me; and I used to think it was so beautiful. I felt really funny with my daughters there listening to it spellbound–just another miniscule layering on of the myths in an especially palatable way. We talked about it a little afterward.''

N.: ''I just don't see it. To me, it's a positive term. I always call my friends 'girls' and I don't see anything wrong with it.''

B.: ''How old are you, N.?''

N.: ''45,'' laughing, ''All right. All right. Let me think about it some more.''

F.: ''I can't imagine a woman executive calling her male secretary, 'my boy,' but in offices you can all be 102 and you're still 'the girls.' Maybe that's how they can get away with all of the rules that say what you can wear, how you should behave, etc. It's easier to discipline 'girls.' ''

P.: ''This is another sort of thing, but maybe it's tied up. What about being called 'honey' and 'baby'?''

D.: ''Well, I resent it if salesgirls call me 'honey,' but that's just a dignity kind of thing. Here they don't know me at all, and they're calling me this ridiculous affectionate term, completely out of any possible context or meaning.''

P.: ''I meant more if your husband or boyfriend calls you 'baby'.''

S.: "Well, I like all those things my husband calls me because he does it with such obvious affection. But I've never thought of possible implications behind them that he might not even be aware of. Now that I think of it, I guess 'baby' could get pretty irritating. I'm not his 'baby': I'm his wife. And though all of us want to be fathered and mothered occasionally, I don't want or need it *all* the time."

G.: "Yes, my husband used to refer to me as his 'fifth girl.' (She has four daughters.) I thought it was cute the first time, and the second time, and then it used to bug me, but I never knew why. Now I see. I was resenting being put in the same class as my little children.

P.: "I was at a party the other night, and a woman patted her husband and said, 'He's just a little boy at heart.' He looked really embarassed, and I thought at the time that it was really a patronizing thing to say."

G.: "Well, I always wanted to stay a girl. Since I've been in the Movement, this is the first time I've wanted to be a woman and I'm really proud of the term. It makes me feel proud and tall and adult. I am a woman. I've gone 360 degrees. Now I'm offended if somebody calls me a girl."

S.: "You've come a long way, baby." (Laughter.)

G.: "Well, like the Hallmark card say, 'All over the world, girls are growing up.'"

Raising consciousness has given me a fresh look at many stale dogmas. The group has taught me many other things also. It has helped me to:

–deal with problems of communication more honestly;

–have a tolerance of different ideas without the urge to change them;

–develop a growing facility in articulation.

In other words, I am learning how to talk to people and how to hear them. Routinely, we encounter many frustrations in our daily lives. Many lie beyond our power to change, like 5 o'clock traffic or crowded stores. But many frustrations could be eased, if we dared face them. Too often, we retreat from these situations, because we want to be nice ("A lady never loses her temper."), although inside we hate them. Sometimes we feel so hostile we are afraid to release the cork. We relieve our frustrations in unrelated ways on uninvolved people. Some of us yell at our kids when we're caught in a traffic jam. We tell a neighbor when a third neighbor has upset us. We merely set up another problem without erasing the first one.

I am learning to deal more honestly with the situations that lie within my control. In one sense, it's getting liberated from myself–from the games I have been taught to play. In a deeper sense, it is intrinsically tied up with female conditioning.

Girls are not taught to be straightforward and

open; they are taught to be devious and manipulating. ("Look at that. Only four years old and already she's wrapping men around her finger. What a charmer!") We wheedle and whine; we trick and manuever. A woman is mysterious. She is unfathomable. By working at it, many of us have reached the zenith of mystery: we are mysterious to ourselves. I am trying to take a little of the mystery out of my life.

At our early meetings, there was a young woman who talked incessantly about herself. She found her navel fascinating, but some of us grew tired of staring at it. We had pretty interesting navels to gaze at also. One week after she had left, I said, "Lynn talks too much." A woman abruptly said, "Don't tell me. Tell her." I was taken aback. Tell *her*? Actually confront her and say, "You talk too much." Why I couldn't do a thing like that. It was impolite. (Better to say hateful things behind her back.)

I thought about it. Initially, I was embarrassed that my "tattle-tale" had been rejected. Then I realized that it was stupid to feel resentment over Lynn's talking, and instead of doing something about it, to go and tell a third person. What I really wanted was for the third person to take my responsibility and fix it up for me. The only sensible response was to communicate with Lynn myself. This was a difficult lesson and I didn't learn it all at once. Little by little, I am improving in telling people about situations that make me uncomfortable.

I have also stopped making excuses for breathing. Women feel they must excuse every action. We are superhuman and can do everything; nothing we do is important enough to make us too busy to do something else. ("Why not call Jane Smith? She's just home all day and I'm sure she'd love to help you out.") We think we should always be on call–be all things to all people. If we can't, we begin to excuse our "lacks." We are always at fault. (How many times today have you said you were sorry?)

Working on the premise that I am a responsible adult, I no longer give fumbling excuses because I choose not to do something. When people call me to collect for something on my block, I say, "No, I'm sorry, but I can't." PERIOD. Then comes this heavy silence while they wait for the excuse, but I no longer fill it. I don't owe them an excuse and they should not expect one. They must grant me the right that I am the only one who can decide the use of my time. It's one of the fringe benefits of being an adult.

Along with learning to talk to people, I've learned to hear them. I grew up a master of the great put-down, skillful in deprecating ideas foreign to my own. I had small tolerance for different ideas because they were a threat to mine. I have discovered that there is no one right route; many ideas and life-styles can stand alongside one another.

Perhaps this is a phenomenon of the times. We have learned well that the melting pot did not melt; only festered, and frustrated and limited. Now I have a willingness and an interest to hear new ideas without a need or desire to change them. They don't threaten mine, nor do they demand a rebuttal.

Some ideas have seemed bizarre to me because I have never heard them before. One woman interpreted Halloween completely in the context of covens of real witches and their ceremonies, about as far from my own "trick or treat" background as possible. Two years ago, I would have thought her crazy. Now I listened and learned something I didn't know. It didn't alter my perception or practice of Halloween, but it did give me a glimpse into someone else's.

This tolerance extends to taboo subjects. In our group, no subject is considered too ridiculous or *verboten* for exploration. During one woman's description of her sexual experiences, my eyes popped slightly with wonder, but they didn't narrow with disapproval. I might not choose her routes, but if I am to know her, I must know and accept what she did. Sex is the hardest subject to be honest about, because it poses the quickest rejection. ("Perverts! All of them!") If one can tell her deepest feeling about sex and be accepted, one can talk about anything.

We had a lesbian in our group, although none of us knew it until she told us. Jeannie had been married, had a child, and didn't give us funny looks. She was making a primary commitment to another woman; we had chosen men—no insurmountable barriers there. She left us to join the Gay Liberation group, which is fighting for equal rights for lesbians. Knowing Jeannie increased my perception of liberation. If one believes in personal choice as a right for *all*, one cannot then make that choice for anybody else. One can't impose her personal concept of freedom on another; that merely substitutes a new bondage. Liberation means everyone must choose for herself what she wants to do with her life. As long as it does not infringe on my rights, I have no reason or right to question it.

I have learned to think again through the weekly discussions. I'm getting smarter every day. My mind lay fallow for many years, and I believed that I had lost the ability to think. This is common among women; we are so fragmented that concentration becomes increasingly difficult. I never could remember "important" things. I would jump into a discussion with flaming emotion and then have my husband bail me out of it with facts and statistics.

The group is gentle with gropings. Though you may know exactly what someone is trying to say, *she* may not know what she is trying to say. It is crucial for one to learn to articulate her frustrations and needs and wants. The only way to learn is to do it. No one ever hurries to finish your sentence or supply your word or interpret for you. Roger always used to say, "I think what Gabrielle means is . . ." and I was very grateful to him for making my fumblings intelligible. Now I am able to make my thoughts intelligible all by myself.

As each of us grows increasingly articulate, much of the four-letter language, common at the beginning, has disappeared. There are many reasons for four-letter language, least important, being inability to articulate. "Swearing" helps one get the rage out faster. At first, when your anger is not in focus, one is unable to exorcise it. One can only grope to express it, and the vehicle chosen for expression is "dirty" words, because they mean anger to us. Swearing is an avowal of freedom, albeit an inconsequential one. When one has little real control over her life, at least she can reject where she's at. She can express a small amount of personal freedom by speaking in a way that is socially unacceptable to the people who are oppressing her. "Unladylike" speech is a quick vehicle for women to proclaim their rejection of the restrictive definition of a "lady."

Another valid reason for swearing is a guarding of privacy. In this media age, everything becomes co-opted in a matter of days. The President says, "Power to the People" without any idea of what it means. He weakens it by giving it his acceptance. The establishment makes a farce of a rebel's feelings by stealing his language and distorting it. The establishment is not going to steal "Fuck you!" so a revolutionary can express rage this way.

Any language is largely a matter of habit. Words frequently used lose their shock value and "foul" words are used as casually as any word or phrase. Sometimes, I still fall into the habit, but I no longer have the need to thumb my nose at anyone in that tiny way. I have enough real freedom in my life now.

In our group, we also talk about what we're going to be when we grow up. Every member has made at least one major change in her life during the past year. We have returned to school, begun careers, severed oppressive relationships. Aspirations are sky-high and we are fulfilling them.

We don't have men come to our group. Many women find it extremely difficult to speak in front of men; they defer to them or are dishonest in their presence. Most men find it difficult to keep quiet and listen without presenting a defense or examples of how they are oppressed too. Of course they are. There are male liberation groups springing up for men to discuss their own oppressions. Ours is for women. (A mixed group also changes the group's focus, switching it to resolving relationships, rather than on developing individual selves.)

Women are our main concern. We look at things in "her" focus. We concentrate on preserving our strengths and strengthening our weaknesses and working together as women. Someday, hopefully, everyone will be able to relate to anyone as people, not as men or women, or roles. Right now we are finding ourselves as women; we are discovering what that means.

"Well, it all sounds lovely, dear, and I'm terribly pleased for you. But so what?"

Well, I'll tell you so what. There are hundreds of these groups all over the country with new ones mushrooming every week. This is not a question of a few people getting together to reinforce their own peculiar perceptions of reality. This is a basic social change and it's happening right now.

Not all of the groups operate in the way I've described ours. That's the point: We are all operating differently because we are different. We won't come up with the right answer because we know now there is no right answer. But we are coming up with many new answers.

The phenomenon of small groups may be only a temporary phase in the movement. At the moment, it is a necessary one: We can't chart a new direction until we know where we are and how we got here. Simultaneously, we are learning to love and respect women and, in the process, to love and respect ourselves. We are also changing the world. Me and my friends.

KINDER, KIRCHEN, KUCHE — KRAP*

CHAPTER 3

KINDER, KIRCHE, KUCHE-KRAP*

Breathes there a woman
With soul so dead
That she actually enjoys
Cleaning the head.**

The first confrontation in most households comes over the housework. It is a major obstacle tripping the woman on the road to anywhere. Even if she works outside the house, she retains primary responsibility for inside it. In our society, housework is woman's work and woman's work is never done.

*Sign carried by a young feminist, during the August 26, 1970, National Day of Strike. The first three K's stand for Children, Church, and Kitchen, a Nazi slogan defining woman's place.
**Poem written by an old feminist, body gnarled and withered by years of dusting rubber plants and ironing Raggedy Ann dresses, but spirit still supple.

Along the route to true femininity, I missed this message. I think housework is creepy, and I give up all genetic claim to it. Some women are able to look at it in "building the cathedral" perspective, but to me, it is always going through the sewer: I was never one who could scrub her toilet, singing little snatches of Rogers and Hammerstein.

Yet I strongly believe in a modicum of order. Roger taught me this, and it was a value painfully acquired. I thought spontaneity was the key to life and casualness a cardinal virtue. When he would suggest that I replace the top of the peanut butter jar, I would wring my hands and say, "How can you possibly experience LIFE when you are so filled with compulsions?" My philosophy was summed up in the simple maxim, "It'll turn up."

When some things didn't turn up until their need had long passed and Roger's compulsions continued to simplify his life, I began to see virtue in his order. If I wanted to spontaneously create a poem, my fervor could diminish in the search for a pencil. Casual entertaining meant that I had to do a crash, heart-attack pick-up before people could plough in. Countless jar tops later, I evolved into a reasonably neat person with a presentable house. But my heart was never in it.

Now I want out. Roger already helps, but I want an equal division of the work and the responsibility. I stumble and mumble through our first talk. Roger ends up resentful. I am frustrated because I can't articulate my feelings persuasively. I say, "WELL! I can measure the extent of my oppression by the extent of your resistance."* It's a great line and gives me a good exit, but the housework stays status quo. It is MY responsiblity.

Roger obviously has a point when he says that he is bringing in the money for the family. Doesn't he? He says it with enough of a huff that momentarily I am A Stricken Ingrate. I retreat to hide my guilt and marshal my arguments. Something doesn't ring true to me.

The whole rationale of work is confused and confusing. Within the framework of the Puritan ethic and societal pressure, there appear to be four compelling reasons men work. There are:

   –those who work because they love it;
   –those who work because of intense ambition and/or compulsion;
   –those who work to keep their families in necessities;
   –those who work to keep their families in luxuries.

These four categories can overlap. In any of them may be the man who works primarily because he has been taught that work is a man's responsibility. As most girls learn to be housewives and mothers, most boys learn to be workers.

*Paraphrase of Pat Mainardi, "The Politics of Housework."

Roger is one of the few fortunate men in the first category. He works because he loves his work. That it simultaneously buys the food is fortuitous, but it's not intrinsic.

We could manage well on half of his annual salary but he is not going to work halftime. Granted his employer wouldn't like it. More to the point, Roger wouldn't like it. This is the fallacy in his protest that he has made his contribution to the household via the paycheck. In reality, he is doing the work he loves, gets well paid for it, and because of it is excused from work he doesn't find fulfilling, i.e., housework. When confronted with this, he reluctantly admits its validity, yet sees no alternative. His career is established; it is satisfying. Someone has to do the housework. It's not feasible for him, although he'll certainly give me a hand with it. In effect, he's saying, "I'm sorry, Gabrielle, but I got there first. You may have made a bad choice, but it looks like you're stuck with it."

Ostensibly, nothing has changed, but he's on the defensive now. I have to be content with this for the moment, and hope that his sense of fairness will start fomenting in my favor.

Some men work to fulfill some inner need, ambition, or compulsion. These men are not thinking primarily of putting bread on the table either. They work inordinate hours, evenings and weekends. They contribute great material comfort to their families, but often it's from guilt over their continued absence, or relief that their families release them with little complaint. There is a thin line between buying one's family color TVs, multiple cars, fur coats and buying OFF one's family.

This type of man may or may not like his work, but it is a tool for him to achieve something he thinks important: a Nobel prize, the presidency of the firm, a lot of money. Human values are subjugated to his personal desires, his career taking precedence over everything. He is allowed to sacrifice his family relationships because he is a man, and in our society, aggressiveness, intense personal ambition, competition, and high achievement are values for men. These same characteristics in a woman would be seen as inexcusably selfish and greatly censured.

When a wife wonders how she can ask her husband to share the housework when he already works a fourteen hour day, she is asking the wrong question. WHY is he working a fourteen hour day? When the husband is incredulous that she could make such a request, in view of his important work, his wonderment is specious and arrogant. His wife could be advancing science and ennobling mankind also were she permitted by training and opportunity. Male sex gives one no corner on contribution. Were the situation reversed with men primarily responsible for child-rearing and housework, the winners of Nobel prizes would be female.

Most men must work primarily to feed their families. Usually they have no choice or control over their jobs because of their immediate needs. Many hate their jobs yet can see no alternatives. Home to these men can be a haven, a release from outside pressures. Should they have to come home and start cleaning house and playing with children? Surely they have done their part. The point is missed here, too. In our affluent society with its professed human values, no one should have to spend a lifetime working a job he hates. If it is a temporary necessity, what dictates that the man must always do it? Why should a man bear the entire economic burden?

When the work is deadening or dehumanizing, what better reason to halve it? If Joe Smith hates his Number 3 assembly line job slot, why not split that job between Joe and Sally Smith. The advantages of splitting a job into half-day or bi-weekly shifts and dividing it between a husband and wife are obvious. The pressures are shared; the father becomes a real presence in raising the children; both partners share the stimulation of the outside world and the security of the home.

Sharing of the same job is radical but feasible. Some jobs might be too physically demanding for some women, but most assembly line jobs do not require great strength, only dulling repetition of the same detail. Employers shouldn't care who does it, as long as the work gets done. The shortened work-week, currently in experiment across the country, where one works four 10 hour days instead of five 8 hour ones, is no less radical and has had very positive results for both employer and employee.

In cases of extreme need, both partners already share the economic burden. Unfortunately, they are often just surviving by doing this, not improving their human existence. Almost always, the woman makes less money than the man. Even if she does identical work, her job is given a different title and the salary lowered.

Women comprise 37% of the labor force and number 32 million;* yet the myth is maintained that work is a hobby for women. Middle class women often perpetuate this myth in an attempt to assuage the psychological burden of proving they are "real" women, even though they work outside the house. "My *important* work is my husband and children. This is just something I do while the kids are in school."

It is a convenient myth for employers, justifying low wages and poor advancement. The myth completes its cycle when it pretends that men need higher wages because they must support a family. Forty-seven percent of the families classified as poor have female heads; 5.6 million of all families

*Women's Bureau, Department of Labor, July, 1971.

in the country are headed by females.* They and the single, ambitious women suffer most from the hobby myth, but it denigrates every working woman's efforts and undermines her value as a contributing member of the society.

Many middle class women never consider the possibility of sharing the economic burden. We have the phenomenon of the well-educated woman who is "so grateful for my Vassar education because it helps me in talking to my husband's friends." A sharing of the physical and psychological pressures upon the middle class man might decrease the high incidence of ulcers and heart attacks among men.

Often the high-ulcer-risk man is one who works a hateful job to keep his family in luxuries. A certain standard of living has been set up and must be maintained. Women acquiesce in this and sometimes actively encourage it. Often the woman pushes the man because she has no other release for her own ambitions. This is why "behind every great man there is a great woman"–pushing him.

Values become twisted with human needs, sublimated into acquisitions. He works longer and

*Robert L. Stein, "The Economic Status of Families Headed by Women," *Monthly Labor Review*, December, 1970.

harder to make more money, and she works longer and harder to fill the void of his absence and her unfulfilled life. Escape pleasures become necessities, the weekend home, the sailboat, exotic vacations. Both do work they hate, and only the escape valves make it possible to continue.

When a woman says, "I couldn't ask my husband to share the housework because he hates his job," they should examine the direction of their lives and consider making changes. Something is wrong if either one or both continue doing things they hate.

Roger and I had long shared the value that if one is lucky enough to have some control, he should not have to work a hated job. He knew that I would move immediately, should his job become unsatisfying. We had never applied the value to me. I had chosen for life.

I was one of the mass of women who ends up performing society's non-profit-making functions. By training girls that their primary job and joy is care of children and a house, society gets these functions performed for free. Even an established professional woman must assume this responsibility. She may delegate it to a housekeeper, but she is expected to hire, fire, supervise, and fill in the gaps. In reality, she if forced to have two full-time jobs. Society gets around this inequity by pretending that housework and child care are not real work. They are beautiful work, but they are not real work.

In our culture, real work is paid work. We measure value by money. If something costs a lot, it must be good or important. ("Wow! Was I sick! The prescription cost $18.00.") Or the converse, ("That medicine couldn't have been too good. It only cost $1.65.") If you do real work, you get paid for it. The more "important" it is, the more you get paid. Housewives get paid nothing. Babysitters and domestics are paid sub-minimum wages. They have no status. Teachers have little status and less money.

When the husband contributes both the money and the status to the family, the wife fares poorly by comparison. She is economically dependent and her self-concept is subtly undermined. She sheepishly says, "I'm just a housewife." She defers to men in important issues and decisions.

One can insist that making a home is the most important job there is; but when no man wants it–when no one will pay for it–and women themselves apologize for it, one is whistling in the wind.

After whistling for eight years, I finally admitted that I had had bad career guidance; I was unhappy in my profession; and I wanted to change my job. I kept garnering my little logics until they presented a decent case. Then I gathered my courage and presented it.

"Roger?" I said.

"Yes, dear?"

"I'd like to talk about something."

"Yes, dear?"

Then I fumbled and mumbled something like this:

"The house is there for the benefit of everyone in the family. The responsibility for it should be divided. At one time in my life, I volunteered to assume everyone's responsibility. It's time for me to be moving on. This will necessitate everyone reassuming his personal responsibility for the functioning of the house."

At this point, you explain that you're going back to school to become a brain surgeon, or write full-time (that's me, saying that), or you're going to raise the kids REALLY without cluttering it up with diverse other full-time gardening, cleaning, or maintenance jobs. If your husband says, "Yeah! And who's gonna pay for all this, sister?" you might point out that a large Eastern bank estimates your annual services are worth $10,000 and you'll deduct your tuition from back wages. But this kind of tit for tat is a dead end route. Either he thinks you're making a contribution and have some personal rights or he doesn't. You might as well find out how the wind blows.

There are some women who truly love being housewives and that's laudable. The whole point of liberation is that everyone makes her own choice. Those women are not reading this book.

There are other women who have eagerly claimed the house as "theirs." Women have so pitifully little that we can call our own, that we brought out of our own efforts or contacts. Most of us get our money, our friends, our status from our husbands. We are pleased to have something be "ours." This is the "Queen of the Castle" syndrome. This is "my" house, "my" kitchen, "my" oregano. If one wants that, fine, but I have gladly relinquished the ownership of the oregano, along with the responsibility for it. Whoever uses it, takes charge of it.

Roger agreed:

–that the house does benefit all of us;

–that a benefit implies a responsibility;

–that if I didn't want to be Queen of the Castle anymore, I should have a right to abdicate;

–that I hadn't shown any great aptitude for housework and eight years was a reasonable trial;

–that I had a right to try something else.

That left us with a big house, four little kids, and one established career. I don't believe in servants so the solution had to be worked out among ourselves. The children are 7, 6, 3, and 7 months,* and we've already been busted twice on child labor laws.

*Editor's note: By publication date, there are five children.

We proceeded to make a schedule. Five jobs are written on slips of paper. On Sunday nights these are shaken in a fish bowl and each person chooses a task for the week. (This silly ceremony is preferred by our kids, who like to feel an element of chance in life. Roger and I would rather throw dice.)

The jobs are recurrent maintenance jobs, the bare necessity to keep the house from collapse. They are:

1. Trash. Empty every wastebasket in the house. Deposit all in outdoor cans daily.

2. Upstairs pick-up. Carry a basket from room to room. Put everything in it that's out of place. Take care of your own things from it. Announce to family that things may now be claimed. There is a one-half hour limit on claiming things, after which they are given away or thrown away.

3. Downstairs pick-up. Same as No. 2, but done on the main floor.

4. Baby. Feed and/or entertain her when parents are busy or tired. Take care of all her things that show up in the pick-up basket. Run and fetch.

5. Bathrooms. Keep from looking like disaster areas. Pick up fallen towels, chip away mounds of toothpaste, a little polishing here and there.

A job is taken for one week, unless one gripes continuously. Then it's taken for two weeks.

The beauty of the schedule is that one only has to do odious tasks once every five weeks. (To each her own odious also. One child shrieks with joy when she draws bathrooms.)

When one completes her task, there is a chart with daily boxes to check. If it is not done, the benefits for that day are forfeited. A benefit is any luxury stemming from membership in the family. For very young children, it may be desserts or television time. For teenagers, it might be use of the family car.

In the beginning, the children required great supervision to complete their tasks. Weary, time-consuming training is necessary. Naturally you can do everything quicker yourself. That's the question: Do you want to go on the rest of your life doing everything?

Even the three year old is now able to do these maintenance tasks satisfactorily. (All right. She's almost four.) That says something about the intelligence required to do most household tasks, but I won't say it out loud in public.

Heavy cleaning is done when absolutely neces-sary. It is divided according to one's capacity. Sometimes, we get up from the dinner table and attack a specific room together, devoting perhaps one-half hour to it. This might occur twice a week. We might spend part of a Saturday morning house-cleaning. Now that Roger is actively involved in the housework, he has lowered his standards.

Polished brass doorknobs and wallpapered closets are esoterica from a bygone era.

The house never has a pristine look. We'd like it to but not enough to pay the price. It would simplify things for us greatly if we could hire a maid. I tried that alternative for a few weeks, but I was unable to handle the situation. Doubtless there are people who can and do maintain a good employment relationship, but ours was unequal. She called me Mrs. Burton, I called her by her first name. No matter how often I requested that she call me Gabrielle, she could not. When I called her by her last name, she thought I was angry.

She asked me to pick her up at her home, and I did. No one picks my husband up for work. He makes a living wage and is expected to provide his own transportation. But I did not pay her a living wage. I was willing to pay her only $2.00 an hour, plus lunch and carfare, the domestic's fringe benefits. That totals $4000 a year, below the poverty level for a breadwinner. The bulk of domestics are the main support of their families.

A domestic should be paid enough money so she doesn't have to accept one's used clothing or used food as fringe benefits. (Maybe she doesn't want that lovely piece of Camembert you're graciously giving her.) She should be responsible for her own transportation. She should be paid a living wage, *after* withholding social security, unemployment insurance, and local, State, and Federal taxes.

64

("Oh, they never declare their earnings anyway."
We force people to be dishonest in order to survive.
She should be paid sick leave and vacation time.
If each of her daily employers set aside one-half
hour wage a working day toward this, the domestic
will have accumulated fifteen days at the end of
a year. This can be used in case of emergency,
sickness, or vacation.

A neighbor of mine asked, "My maid had a
death in her family and couldn't come. What are
the ethics of paying her?" Another quickly replied,
"I don't believe in paying for work that isn't done."
Rubbish! We believe in it for our husbands. We
call it annual leave, sick leave, emergency leave.
We demand it. But our husbands do important
things. We don't believe in these benefits for domestics because they don't deserve it. Housework is
not important; we are unwilling to pay for it.

Many women also use domestics for babysitters, without increasing their wages. They plan
a full day, disappear the moment she arrives, and
then complain bitterly about the quality of work
performed. Yet every woman knows how difficult it is to work with small children underfoot.

If one can't pay a higher wage, isn't it still
better to do what one can? Otherwise so many
people would be unemployed. This is always the
argument advanced to buy more time. Situations
never improve until people decide to be just. At
this time, I am unable to pay what I consider

just. If I pay the going rate, it would be oppressing someone to free myself. We made the mess; we will take responsibility for it.

One reason we have so much mess is that we are inundated with possessions. Possessions can become a pain in the neck. The labor of upkeep can quickly suffocate the pleasures of possession.

Some things show up in the pick-up basket that no one cares enough about to take responsibility for. In the past, I would have said, in a long-suffering voice, "That beautiful thing. Tsk! Tsk! I'll do it," for I was Woman The Conserver. Now I throw it out or give it away.

At first I thought we had too many possessions because we spent too much money. It's not as simple as that. Financially secure people are almost forced to continually consume because of the lack of community in our society. America has become one vast anti-community. In the cities, people barricade themselves behind their locked doors and complicated buzzing systems. The new high-rises resemble fortresses. In the suburbs, people fiercely guard their "independence." While this may keep out burglars and busybodies, it has the drawback of also keeping out people.

Lack of community means isolation, and the isolated man must prepare for every contingency. Though we live jammed on top of one another, we equip ourselves like the last house on the open frontier. We all buy the same possessions, put them in our private corners, and polish them alone. We fear that communal ownership will infringe on our privacy or good nature.

A few years ago, Roger approached neighbors about the possibility of pooling money and buying common lawn mowers. We all have huge yards, and he foresaw sharing the many necessary garden tools. Everyone thought it was a great idea, but no one wanted to do it. All were afraid that no one would be responsible or trustworthy enough. Every family now has between 100 and 500 dollars invested in a mower that is used once a week. There are dozens of duplications like that—washing machines, waffle irons, power drills—the luxuries that have become necessities because we don't trust in community. I value privacy greatly, and owning something communally is not going to rob me of it. There would be specific details to arrange in advance but nothing too taxing for the human intellect. In return, one could gain leisure (from not polishing), money (from not buying), space (from not storing), and a bit of community. I'm willing to chance my waffle iron on that.

The discoveries that possessions were complicating our lives and lack of community was penalizing us, came months after the initial housework confrontation. At first, I flew blind, guided only by a desire to change my life and knowing I couldn't, bogged down by housework. It didn't go as smoothly as the retelling sounds. It was often desultory, sometimes hostile, and never easy. In the beginning, I went around burdened with guilt. What right did I have to make all this commotion just to be happy? That passed in exact proportion to the increase in my happiness. When one is happy, one no longer questions her right to it. One just enjoys it.

There were some things that were very difficult for me to ask of Roger, like cleaning the bathrooms. For crying out loud, he is a PhD, and I am just a housewife. It was more fitting for me to do it.

I did it for several months. One night, I slipped it into the conversation that he was still sheltered from the harsher realities of housework. He said he could manage to swipe a toilet occasionally and even mop a hairy floor. Seems he had done it in his Army days (for punishment). "But you haven't done it in years," I protested. "It's like bicycling," he said. "It's not a skill one easily forgets." He picked up the Bon Ami and became a full participating member of this cooperative.

Changing stereotyped roles is a difficult ongoing process. The solidarity of my weekly W.L. discussion group gave me the courage to begin the process and to persevere. When I would encounter roadblocks, we would discuss them in the group and tackle the solutions together.

Some roadblocks come from within women ourselves. We are so conditioned by training and environment that we are fearful to attempt change or are willing to settle for small tokens.

You will get what you ask for. One's husband is a product of his conditioning also. Intellectually, he may be ready for women's liberation but emotionally, your wants may be very difficult for him. This is why YOU must initiate the confrontations. If you want a sharing of the household responsibilities, you must ask for it. He is not going to bring it up. He has time to lose and uninteresting work to gain. He must reappraise his ideas of what constitutes masculinity and femininity, an easy intellectual exercise, somewhat more difficult when one is wearing an apron.

If you do not attempt to change your life, you have no chance. A lot of women are afraid to ask. They have a realistic fear of making themselves unlovable by pushing too much. When one is totally dependent upon one person, it doesn't pay to annoy that person too much. Still, your self-worth and self-confidence will never increase until you have time to develop yourself.

Most women experience the conflict I showed with the bathrooms. Covertly, they think they really are inferior to their husbands. He has more important things to do. So will you.

Many say, "Well, my husband already helps me out a lot." That may be true, but the philosophy behind it is usually wrong. He's helping you with *your* work, the children are helping mamma with *her* work. Ultimately *you* are still responsible for it.

Some women are very unhappy as housewives but don't know what else they could do. Perhaps they have never been trained for anything they like. Maybe they don't know *what* they like. When financial circumstance permits, a woman should have the same trial-and-error searching periods that many men do. If she tries something and finds she doesn't like it, she should be allowed to experiment further, until she discovers and develops herself. Men often change jobs several times before they settle. Some never settle. Women have a one-shot chance. It may be disastrous, but it's final.

In the attempt to give me a second chance, we have evolved the current division of responsibilities. It is not a permanent solution. We are trying to break away from feeling that everything must be permanent in our lives. Permanency is not necessarily synonomous with stability and maturity. It can just as easily become a fake fortress hiding stagnation and fear. The true test of a solution should be whether it meets one's particular needs at a particular time. People have different needs and desires at different periods in their lives. No one would expect a person to be irrevocably bound by her age 17 philosophy. Why should ages 25, 35, or 50 be any more sacred?

Our arrangement is working satisfactorily now; in a year it may be unsuited to our needs. In the future we might use a professional housecleaning service on a weekly contractual basis, for that seems to combine personal dignity with efficiency. Perhaps we might gravitate to an extended family relationship with an even further division of responsibilities. But those are tomorrow's decisions.

I am mentally liberated from housework. I still do some, as we all do, because it is there. What I do, I resent less, because it is no longer the sole reason for my being. Except for my scheduled tasks, I feel no personal responsibility or guilt for work undone. It is probably true that if the house were in a state of collapse and somebody walked in, they wouldn't say, "Roger sure keeps a messy house." But not very many of those people drop in anymore.

CHAPTER 4

WHAT A LIVING DOLL!

She: "I was just thinking about how it all started."
He: "What's that, sweetheart?"

In the main, to be a woman is to be an image. Some of us are many images. Certain images have more prestige than others. The most prestigious image is the Madonna.

Not all images are available to women, some being reserved "for men only." In medicine a woman could easily achieve a Nightingale image, but never a Ben Casey one.*

An image should never be confused with an identity. Many images do not add up to one self. Most women are not aware of this distinction.

*Of course a man who achieves the Nightingale image ("He has *such* tender hands–a real angel.") might have a little trouble with society, too. This is not exclusively a female problem. Men are also crippled by stereotypes.

If a woman is a good image, she may become an object, i.e.:

    a. a thing;

    b. a possession;

    c. (Philos.) that which is seen only in relation to a subject.

Clever women can qualify for all three categories.

If a woman is a good object, she can cultivate new images. For instance, a successful sex object has a greater chance of achieving the image of "desirable wife." ("The girl that I marry will have to be/As soft and as pink as a nursery.")

It's a very complex business being a woman. This is part of why we're so goddam mysterious.

I am WOMAN. Gaze into my ever-changing well of surprises. I am PTA mother in my brown wren dress, Saturday night swinger in my satin hot pants, homemaker in my perma-press housedress. The girl in me still peeks through my pleated skirt and knee socks; I am my husband's mistress in my black negligee. I have a facade—an image—a role for every occasion. If you or I get tired of "me," I have only to change my lipstick, flip my wig, buy a new dress.

Our society defines the fulfilled woman's role as a married-mother. Marriage alone is not sufficient. Childless couples are continually badgered to reproduce. Maternity alone does not satisfy society, only angers it.

Every female person regardless of qualifications or personal preference, is pressured into this "married-mother" direction. Those who accept it are regarded as "normal," "true" women. Those who fight it are regarded with pity ("Isn't it a shame a nice girl like you never got married?"), with scorn ("bitch," "shrew," "nag"), as failures ("frustrated old maid"). A few women are allowed to sublimate their "natural destiny" if they don't deny it, as is the case with nuns, who become "spiritual mothers."

Society has a partial tolerance for women who choose other roles–we have our quotas for female doctors and lawyers–but these women are still considered "lacking" if they don't perform the "married-mother" role simultaneously. ("Such a brilliant doctor. She would have made a wonderful mother.")

Since the roles open to women are so severely limited, many women have confused role with identity–i.e., filling the role is the same as being a person. A role is only a part one performs or a function one assumes.

Every role has its images, the symbolic or figurative representations of it. For example, the role of mother is multi-imaged. It includes:

1. The Madonna;
2. The Nurse, wiper of wounds and succorer of psyches;

76

3. The Cook–"Nothin' says lovin' like something from the oven;"
4. The Civic Leader–active in PTA, the Brownie troop;
5. The Homemaker–a good mother dresses her family in "whiter than white" laundry.

BUT: neither role nor image is the person–the self–the identity; each is only part of the myriad dimensions making up a person. Women show their puzzlement over this distinction by saying sincerely, "I only want to be a good wife and mother," and simultaneously crying out, "I want to be more than Joey's mother–Ed's wife–Rover's mistress. I want to be *me*.

But what is "me?" How does one get to be "me?" Those of us who searched for "me" in certain roles and images have ended up only with roles and images that become obsolete as circumstances and environment change.

Most of us were taught that "me" lies in another person. We had only to find our "other half" to complete us. "I'm Mrs. So-and-So, Charlie's wife." This goal can be temporarily satisfactory unless something happens to Charlie. If Charlie dies, one can shift to being "Charlie's widow," a new role-image. But what if Charlie divorces "me" or worse yet, withdraws psychologically? Many women who settled for this answer to their "being" have shared the experience of feeling frightened for their "existence" when their

Charlies have excluded them. "I felt as if I weren't there–as if I were nothing." This is also expressed in: "I feel as if I only exist for other people;" or "When the children left, I had no more reason for being." In some cases, they *are* nothing, for when one depends totally upon a relationship for her identity, a cessation or altering of that relationship can cease the identity.

Many women continually look into mirrors. Ostensibly this is a female vanity and certainly reflects a preoccupation with image. But sometimes it is more: a search for identity–a tangible proof of existence. If one shows, one must be.

Women are noted for their indulgence in hysterics–tantrums. "Look at me. Pay attention to me. Listen to me." If no one sees you, can you really be there? Be? (This has an obvious corollary in the black experience. For centuries, blacks have been "invisible.")

Women come by this "identity crisis" naturally. Our way of living systematically separates females from their identities. We teach females to aspire to "roles" or "images" instead of to develop themselves as people. Girls are told to react, rather than act. Passivity is a feminine virtue; activity is masculine. We subtly introduce the idea that a strong self is tantamount to aggressiveness. Casually we say, "Don't be *yourself* so much. Listen to what your boyfriend–fiancé –husband is saying."

All these things contribute to females having weak or confused self-concepts. In our society, there are several "good" reasons for doing this. All are intertwined with maintaining an ever-increasing consumer economy. Great parts of our economy are directly dependent upon women having a weak self-concept. A multi-billion dollar fashion-cosmetic industry testifies to the validity of this approach. A woman who does not know who she is can be sold anything. She can also be used as a shill to sell anything.

Employers prey upon the weak self-concept of women in order to exploit them as a disposable labor force. Only people who feel that they are, in truth, exploitable–expendable–of low value–can be exploited. The economy can absorb just so many workers without profits being cut. If large segments of the population consider themselves expendable, they can be used when the need arises, as in wartime, when women took over "men's" jobs, and expended when the need disappears. They can be dissuaded from even entering the labor force to "compete" with men if they are convinced that their real role–real value–lies in taking care of their husbands and children. A woman staying home and maintaining the "necessities" of life becomes a prime consumer, frees a worker (the man) to continue contributing to the economy, and raises a new generation of workers cost-free.

The cycle completes when parents and teachers perceive the status quo (accurately) and perpetuate it by training children to adjust. We call this process socialization, and it goes like this:

THANK HEAVEN FOR LITTLE GIRLS: "Well, one nice thing about having a little girl is dressing her up in all those ribbons and ruffles. It's kinda like playing dolls."

Most parents do dress little girls up like dolls. We start early making decorative objects out of them–things to be admired. Scant thought is given to the psychological and physical restrictions of most girls' clothing. Routinely, we say, "Now don't get your pretty dress dirty. Just play with your dolls or something quiet." Automatically, climbing trees, exploring nature, everything but passive play, is eliminated. Then we exclaim, "Isn't it amazing! Little girls are so gentle and docile and little boys are so rough." Throughout this time, books, games, and toys repeat a subtle message to little girls. Almost without exception, they show females in a variety of servile or decorative roles.

There is a nether period in between late childhood and pubescence during which most parents don't overtly condition their daughters. There are those over-anxious mothers who have their girls in "training" brassieres by age ten and gauze their little stick legs in "grown-up" hosiery on the same shopping trip. But the average girl-child is not expected to go into serious training until age twelve. We are a civilized people with values after all.

PUBERTY AND ADOLESCENCE: The pressure commences. A permissive parent may have allowed "tomboyishness" up to this point, but here we start in earnest to separate the girls from their identities. Now our attitudes toward females shine clearly. We push the boys to be "subjects" ("Get out there and stick up for your rights." "Make the team." "Maintain your grades." "Aggress." "Compete.") We sit on the girls to be "objects" and to serve. ("Well, somebody's got to do the dishes, and it's more important for your brother to achieve." "Sit with your knees together." "How do you expect to get a husband?" "Baby-sit." "Be a little mysterious." "Go to charm school.")

The pubescent girl quickly perceives that in our culture, a female's value lies in her body, both as a reproductive tool and as a reservoir of pleasure. All adolescents are caught up in the body craze to some extent, but the focus is different. In young boys, the body is generally the means to the end; in young girls, the body *is* the means and the end. Males develop muscles to make the football team or become astronauts. Females groom bodies to attract the athlete and budding scientist.

The girl is pressured to turn her body into a sex object in order to achieve the sanctioned role of wife-mother. This is a tricky line for young girls to straddle. One wants to be "sexy" enough to attract without becoming *too* sexy, thus turning into one of those girls "they go around with but won't marry." A neighbor of mine expressed this in grown-up reference after seeing Raquel Welch in person, "She was fantastic–an incredible body– and I had all kinds of fantasies. On the other hand, I wouldn't really want to bring her to a PTA meeting. She was so *hard*."

IMAGES I ASPIRED TO IN ADOLESCENCE:

1. The All-American girl. This would be a stepping stone to No. 2.
2. Miss America.
3. Norma Janis, the most popular girl in my high school, a vapid pretty girl with sausage-curled hair, who rode around in a white convertible.*
4. Kim Novak, coming down the stairs in *Picnic*.
5. Audrey Hepburn.

Rather modest heroines I had, and even then I never realized one of my aspirations, though I devoted endless time, thought, and money to the pursuit. The only one I came close to was No. 5. I thought I *was* that one after I lost twenty pounds. Looking back at photos of that period, I looked

*N.J. is now a faded housewife with three kids and a chronically unfaithful husband who berates her in public for being dumb. She cries.

like Mrs. Munster in sunglasses. My souvenir of that image is permanent eye-damage from wearing dark glasses day and night for two years.

All of my teenage heroines were sex objects, of varying degrees of obviousness. I had never heard of women who *did* anything–not for me an Elizabeth Blackwell (the first woman doctor in the U.S.) or a Maude Gonne. Who?*

Most heroines available to young girls are either sex objects (movie stars, models, airline stewardesses) or appendages to famous men, heroic by proximity. Look at the ten most admired women annually. Almost without exception, they are *wives* of someone famous.

AGONIES ALONG THE ADOLESCENT ROAD TO BECOMING A SUCCESSFUL SEX OBJECT IN ORDER TO BECOME A SUCCESSFUL ROLE/ IMAGE: In our country, we are big on breasts. We are absolutely queer on them. If we had a national shield, we could emblazon this motto on it: "It's what's up front that counts."

I had breasts, thank God, but I paid my dues in this club.

Age 11: Four members of my gang are sitting around a kitchen table and one girl classifies us as "fruits." Marietta is a grapefruit. Sharon is an orange, Carol is a lemon, and Gabrielle is

*M.G. was an Irish revolutionary.

a seed. The seed laughs, then excuses herself to flee home and devote days to sobbing. (Footnote learned years later: the grapefruit, secretly mortified by her pneumatic wealth, sobs in private also. She is terrified that she'll never stop growing and will end up grotesque. She copes by rounding her shoulders and wearing obscuring clothes.)

Age 12: A "disgusting" eighth grade boy amuses himself by snapping girls' brassieres. The seed lives in fear that he will discover that she still wears undershirts. Each morning she carefully rolls her pink nylon baby garment into a narrow band to simulate the tell-tale strap of prestige.

Age 13: The seed goes into J.C. Penney's-grabs a bra from a table-rushes into a dressing room-and fumbles it on. When a saleswoman offers help, she blushes wildly and stammers, "No." She leaves it on, pays for it, and runs home. At nightfall, she hides it under her mattress.

But in her haste and shame, she has chosen a 34C, and she is indeed a seedling. Behind her locked door, she rips out the binder, her fat, little girl fingers remaking it with big clumsy stitches. She ends up with two glompy pieces of material strung on straps. It bunches under her clothes and surely looks peculiar, but by god, it is a brassiere.

Age 15: All the trauma is not in vain. The seeds ripen and bring their just rewards. When she takes them down the street, boys and men assess them and throw accolades at their owner. ("Will you look at the build on that one?") At parties, males will gather around and look at them.

Age 16: Further victory. The seed is Homecoming Queen and is paraded around a football field–past the lemon, the orange, and the grapefruit. But this triumph is bittersweet. Photos shot of her from the bleachers later reveal cleavage–not just a delicate hint of cleavage but great, gulping, heaving chasms. The nuns censor the photographs but not before everyone has ogled the black and white exposure. The seed becomes religious and doesn't wear sweaters for three years.

Age 17: She has a summer job as a waitress. On her first day, the manager chucks her under the chin and gives her kindly advice, "Stick out those boobs and go out there and get those tips." She is a terrible waitress but the tips roll in.

Age 18: A nun in a physiology course teaches the advantages of breastfeeding. The former seed sits there in her blouse, thinking, "How wonderful! To have a reason for the damn things that makes sense." In her experience they have been used for everything else except this. Later her enthusiasm will temper when she is patronized by modern doctors ("Now, my dear, are you trying to *prove* something?"), censored by other women for being "primitive," and shut up in a back room by Society. Numerous social occasions will find her nursing the baby in "solitude" (i.e., secrecy) while the conversations continue below. Nursing in public is disgusting.

So goes the normal development of the American adolescent female. Unless you were a girl, you cannot imagine the agonies breasts cause. Those who want them devote hours to tedious pectoral exercises, send away $9.95 to Mark Eden for "guaranteed" breast developers, buy rubber fakes, even have plastic inserted into their bodies at great expense, pain, and physical risk. All this to join their well-endowed sisters and become eligible to have pimply boys grab at you, men in subways rub up against you, grown men meet your breasts before they meet your eyes.

In the face of staggering world problems and desperation, the size of breasts is not fit stuff for trauma. The absurdity of it boggles one, yet this is the stuff we allow and subject females to. Society sets certain standards, and one's life must be arranged around them.

We aren't even consistent in our great freak-out over breasts. The rules keep changing and the clever girl must keep up with them or lose the prize. A few of the current regulations are:

1. A big bust is desirable–is sexy–indeed almost mandatory, but only in private or semi-private. In public, the damn things should be kept down.
    a. Jiggling is out.

b. Flopping is not cool.

2. The natural look is in vogue, but only if achieved by unnatural means, i.e., the non-bra that reveals the *real* you. "Now the bra for those women who want the bra-less look!"

a. The real, *real* you is only permitted if you're small or firm.

3. Well, not *too* small. If you're too small, people won't love you. "Dear Ann Landers, I am getting married and am scared to death to tell my fiance' that I wear falsies . . ."

4. Topless go-gos are cool.

5. Cleavage is cool, except in church or business offices.

6. Businessmen eating lunch with bared paps at eye-level is cool.

7. Nursing in public is disgusting.

The whole thing must be governed with a sense of dignity.

We are very big on propriety, and our sense of fitness is not restricted to the pectoral area. Moralists may protest, but there is often a correlation between modesty and body build.

We profess a tolerance of deviations in this country, but we only pay lip service to it. Actually, deviations from our accepted norms offend and/or irritate us. This is most obvious in the way we treat minority groups—"Give me your huddled masses yearning to breathe free, but for god's sake hurry up and learn the language—merge into the common denominator–and don't go around like a bunch of foreigners." It also peeks through in our attitudes toward the body. The body that is not beautiful should be covered up.

Deviations may be revealed in semi-private places, like burlesque houses ("Miss 48"), used in back-seats of cars ("She was a real dog, but put a bag over their heads and they're all the same."), and ogled in pornographic magazines ("You have never seen anything like *this*!")–but decent folks have a right to be protected from that sort of thing.

Americans abroad the first time often express amazement at the numbers of fat and/or old women in bikinis on the public beaches. Europeans are certainly aware that some bodies are more pleasing than others but though they reward their Brigitte Bardots, they don't penalize others for not fitting into that mold. Their more sensible approach says, "If you'be got it, that's nice, but in the end, a body is only a body."

We say we think that, but practice reveals our schizophrenic attitude: A male friend and I were parked, waiting for the signal to change. A young girl strode by our car. She had huge breasts, unfettered by a brassiere, and she was flopping in every direction. He said, "Now is she liberated or just doesn't she know any better?"

Overheard at a party: "I don't mind small-breasted girls running around without underwear. But it's the big, pendulous ones who are doing it–the ones who really *need* a bra."* The speaker was a woman.

A newspaper squib that Lane Bryant would carry "hot pants" in sizes to 52 brought great reader response to this "horror" story.

What we really say is: "Flippety girls, don't you dare jiggle down public streets–unless your build is perfect!" "Fat people, if you must get hot in summer and go outside in daylight, at least have the decency to cover yourself up!"

Our eyes are too tender from their constant exposure to media-made Beauty. We know what is Beauty. We have sacrificed females on its altars.

The discovery of Beauty is not haphazard. One takes the total immersion course during adolescence and spends years after in refresher courses. We are pressed, programmed, defined, wrung, plucked, scraped, and squirmed into passing molds.

All this I learned from age twelve to age eighteen: to be sexy enough to attract, but not sexy enough to repel or be exploited too soon. One must gauge her market value and how to

---

*Regardless of what brassiere manufacturers are hysterically saying, there is no physiological reason for most women to wear a bra. Many women do prefer support for strenuous sports. I, for instance, take tennis very seriously; still I see no reason to beat my breast over it. If you think that hanging appendages need constant support, the men's boxer shorts market is in trouble.

wisely invest her favors. After my breasts developed, I was free to work on my hips, posture, smile, and body odor. No facet of my body could afford to be overlooked or *I* might be overlooked.

Other girls were my natural enemies. There was one grand prize–male attention–and all other females were my competitors for it. Competition is healthy for business. If Sally wows the boys in the latest fashion, Jane can't afford to pass it up.

Meanwhile, back at the socialization process:

By LATE TEENS TO EARLY TWENTIES: I had turned into quite an attractive object, and I had a few good images going for me. At this time, marriageable age, the fight gets overtly dirty; no more soft sell because time is running out. You've already had your nose bobbed, your chest siliconed, and your armpits and legs depilatoried. Oh, you had your mustache removed at the same time; that was good. You own four synthetic wigs and human hair eyelashes and plastic fingernails PLUS a padded girdle to give you that "walk-away oomph." And you still haven't got a man? Well, I hate to tell you this, but your vagina stinks. BUY PRISTINE.

If you're clever, conscientious, and lucky, that wonderful day will arrive when you achieve the prettiest image of all, the

BRIDE: Now there's a business for you (5 billion dollars annually). It's only unfortunate that it self-destructs. But cheer up, image exploiters! The horizons are even wider, for every bride will automatically turn into a

HOMEMAKER: the biggest image of them all. Whatever role you dream up, they are dying to buy. All those women pressed into a limited role are desperately trying to make it into something big enough to fill a life. You can plumb their guilts (Why aren't they happy–is there something wrong with *them*?)–then offer them remedies (Your family and you will be happier if you only buy *insert anything here*). For starters, there's:

–the gracious HOSTESS image: she needs gourmet cookbooks, imaginative table settings, at-home hostess gowns.

–the MISTRESS image: for "wives should always be lovers, too." She needs negligees, martini shakers, and matching designer sheets and pillowcases.

–the REFUGE image: she needs furniture and food and clothes so she can properly succor the bruised survivor of the business-world rat-race.

–the MAINTAINER OF LIFE'S NECESSITIES: she needs washing machines, the best detergents, and every work timesaver so she can dispense with the work and concentrate on being a, b, and c.

And before one can say Jolly Green Giant, the little woman will be standing there crushing her leftover cereal crumbs for casserole toppings; and suddenly she will realize that she's going to be a

MOTHER: and it begins again. A whole new generation to direct and define and coincidentally, get rich on. Oh joy!*

So goes the image/role business. In the past, advertisers and the media were limited to *reflecting* the tastes, fashions, and life-styles of our culture, now they have the power to *make* them. In cases where new fashions and life-styles begin spontaneously–as in the hippie culture–they jump on the bandwagon to exploit them. This the beauty of the business. No one is immune.

HIPPIE: "Wanted! A groovy, well-built chick to share pad and expenses." The hippie woman is very vulnerable to exploitation. She gives all for a possible nothing; the married-mother at least gets a home and security. To the entrepreneur, the hippie means a whole new market–leather, fringe, sandals, and peace paraphernalia.

LIBERATED WOMAN: A current restaurant ad sniffs out the trend and proclaims: "Liberate your wife. Take her out to dinner tonight."

There is no end to the money that can be made from using people who have a weak self-concept or have been limited to find fulfillment

*Roles and images can conflict. A new mother was concerned over what to wear on her first public appearance after childbirth. She wanted to show that she had her figure back–thus available again as a "sex object"–without detracting from her newly acquired "Madonna" image.

in one "destiny"–and who are told that their lack of fulfillment lies in themselves, not the "destiny." People who have never learned who they are can be led in any direction, and all directions make money.

Someplace along the road to getting to their "destiny," many women get lost. They lose their *selves*, in the constant shucking on and off of stereotyped roles and images. Many women appear to function well in and through their series of images, but underneath the facades, the foundations are shaky. It is a risky business to limit a person to a role, and some of us don't want anything more to do with it.

Not that the beginning liberationist doesn't have a little trouble with images, too. *What* does one wear to her first orientation meeting? Too sloppy might indicate that one is a slob and couldn't really make it as a sex object; too neat might mean that one is still a fashion slave. Perhaps a safe choice might be Lord and Taylor blue jeans? Then one goes through a dishevelled period; as her consciousness raises, she dresses scruffy to show she's nobody's decorative object anymore. But years of uncertainty leave their mark. "I couldn't help it. I felt really creepy. I was the only woman in the whole place with short hair." or "Well, I don't mind a little fringe under my arms and on my legs. It's going around with this damn mustache that's killing me." As one starts getting a sense of self and freedom, one wears what one pleases, shaves or doesn't as she decides. This is part of liberation—freedom from an image defined by someone else.

If girls are judged almost exclusively on their faces and figures, i.e., as objects, women are judged on the same scale with more sophisticated measuring instruments.

"I'm so proud to be seen with you on my arm."

"You are a real decoration to this gathering."

"Is she a positive asset to her husband? Have a pleasing appearance?"

"Has she let herself go?"

In our culture a man's sexual value is defined by a combination of his dimensions: his personality, talents, intelligence, earning power, and physical appearance. A woman rests her case for sexual value almost entirely on her physical appearance. When she is middle-aged, she is barred from the sexual image and confined to asexual images and roles. Cary Grant in his sixties stars opposite a constant stream of twenty and thirty year olds. The age disparity is never alluded to. It is usual for a man to marry a woman ten to fifteen years his junior, particularly if it is his second marriage. When a woman does the same, she is the butt of obscene jokes. A man in his forties is at his peak, a woman has plummeted and had better resign herself to civic duties, volunteer work, or better yet, her grandchildren.*

*Inge Powell Bell, "The Double Standard," *Transaction,* (November-December, 1970).

The question is often asked. "Just whatta you women want anyway?" This is one thing we want: to define ourselves. I am not certain what it means to define oneself or how one does it, but I am dead sure that its essence doesn't lie in infantile and exploitable stereotypes. I have lived all the images and performed a good many of the roles. I found some of them very enjoyable but I didn't find any of them sufficient for a life.

It is more than mastering certain "tricks of the trade." It is wrong to enjoy being a girl because one is good at it–because one is a competent charmer and is allowed power through cajolery. "When you look at me with those big brown eyes, Gabrielle, I couldn't refuse you anything."

It is hindered by semantic put-downs like "doll," "baby," or "chick,"* and insidious statements like, "They sound like a bunch of suburban housewives." No person is so simple or small or unimportant to be confined to a role or image.

I think that one can find the elusive "me" only by discarding the accumulated images and

---

*The remark is often made, "I understand your wanting daycare centers and equal pay but you dilute your case when you talk about unimportant things, like the usage of 'doll,' 'baby,' or 'chick'." If they're so unimportant, stop using them. Thoughtless semantics can be the most viable weapon in perpetuating prejudice because well-intentioned people use them. Think of calling a Negro "boy," " jewing someone down," "japping someone" and then tell me "doll" is only your way of showing endearment.

putting one's roles into perspective. A mirror will not reflect the answer. The image is *not* the person. A role is only a part of the whole. One must follow up the hints of where unique potential talents lie–explore new areas and ideas–see what feels right and brings pleasure, once the externals are stripped.

When I walk down the streets these days, no one turns around to stare in awe. They never did in the past either–the difference is that I always wanted them to. Now I am interested in what I think I am and what I might become. To be just a person. Just me.

CHAPTER 5

THE DEMANDS

ABORTION
CHILDCARE CENTERS
EQUAL PAY FOR EQUAL WORK

***

THE DEMANDS

ABORTION

The most loaded issue in the whole Women's Movement is abortion. Both advocates and opponents find themselves unable to discuss it dispassionately without an adrenalin-surging collision of religious and moral trainings, heart-rending experiences of unwanted pregnancies, and general tender feelings about babies. As a practicing Catholic of Irish background, I particularly approach the subject with trepidation.

The issue is basic to any striving for liberation because it must come to terms with the whole question of a person's right of self-determination—when and if a woman qualifies for this right—and whether any true liberation will ever be possible if women are denied the right to control their bodies, especially their reproductive organs. I set my discussion of it on my personal cultural and religious grounds for they have been the ones I've had to traverse in making my own decisions.

Well-trained Catholics have never been particularly equipped or comfortable in dealing with moral decisions because of lack of practice. Traditionally, we have been willing, even eager, to let others make our decisions for us. One only had to ask the parish priest who could flip to the proper page and find the correct answer. Small matter to me when I was accused of suffering brainwashing gladly–I had the consolation that the buck was passed and if responsibility would descend, it wasn't going to descend on me. That consolation is worth a whole bunch of relinquished freedom.

Many religious establishments have assumed this responsibility for their members and it's only recently that some people have decided that they want this no more. When self-determination becomes a value and a necessity, it opens up a whole can of worms. It means that one must sort out each decision with fresh perspective and honest examination and be willing to bear the consequences of "free will." Well, I've passed that hurdle and part of my current Worms contains the morality or immorality of abortion.

In accepting the concept of "free will" and its necessary consequences, "reform" Catholics have had to overcome two problems. The first is getting over a paranoia of persecution; the second is sorting out the indiscriminate indoctrination that this has led to.

Historically, Catholics have had their share of persecution. Though no one has thrown us to the lions for some time, there have been subtler forms practiced, most recently during the great wave of Irish emigres into America. The persecution was perceived accurately–Catholics were kept out of jobs and suffered blatant discrimination–but the reasons for it were inaccurately attributed. Perspective now enables us to see that discrimination ensued mainly because of the real economic threat that the hordes of Irish presented, but try and tell that to my great uncle Patrick, and he'll scoff you the whole way to the saloon. Most Irish were convinced that the heathens were out to get them. God knows there are few temperaments that can be more insufferable than Irishmen who sniff a battle. Their defense mechanisms took the form of protesting not only their equality–they stiffened their backs and their righteousness and went one step further, saying in effect, "We are not only different. We are *better*!" They banded together for strength, raced to form ghettos to protect their children from the pagans' threat, and made up an abundance of rules to increase the exclusiveness of their particular club.

Often when a threat occurs to a culture, a minority of spokesmen and leaders emerges and the majority defers to them willingly. The Irish chose the clerics to be their high priests, while they concentrated on preserving their identity by becoming more Irish than those back on the Emerald Isle, and more Catholic than the original apostles.*

---

*This is not a unique phenomenon either. Several years ago, I became friendly with an Israeli couple who were spending a year in the U.S. They were very

The high priests accepted the offered power gladly and met the threat of "keeping the faith" by codifying and enforcing a huge body of rules. That's a valid defense–to maintain rigid codes as protection from insidious influences–but the rules became entwined with superstitions and myths and gradually all took on a sameness in necessity and seriousness. Punishments were meted out with indiscriminate severity also, as there simply weren't enough punishments to go around. One could burn in hell for eating meat on Friday, getting drunk on Saturday, or missing Mass on Sunday. Murder drew the same sentence.

It is perfectly valid for an institution to impose rules of behavior on its members. In a theological sense, these rules constitute a kind of morality and are binding upon anyone who buys into the particular system. But there are different levels of morality and the Church made her error by not distinguishing among them–merely lumping them all under one large umbrella. This simplistic approach made no distinction between morality-by-Church-edict and more universally recognized moral principles, such

religious, keeping a semi-kosher home, always observing the Friday evening Shabbat. After some months, they told me that at home in Israel, they barely practiced their traditions, feeling no need to. There, all were Jews and so there was no problem with a sense of identity. Coming to an "alien" culture, they chose to revert to the old traditions in order to keep a sense of who they were.

as incest prohibition. (Whether such universal principles automatically emanate from human nature or from evolutionary experience is not at issue here.) To eat or not to eat meat on Friday was a valid Church-imposed edict and should not have been regarded as being more. Fasting during Lent, compulsory attendance at Mass, the prohibition of having one's palm read, are all similar examples of confused moral matters.

No one bothered to point out that the Catholic Church varied from country to country. Many mentors sincerely believed that "a little knowledge quickly became a dangerous thing" and declined to bother their charges with piddling distinctions that would only lead to confusion and temptation.

I remember sitting in a convent in the West Indies–a grown woman then–eating a piece of bread at a fancy Friday luncheon, while all around me, other guests were blandly chomping meat. Though the meat was being served by *nuns*, I quietly passed it all by–no mortal sin for me, regardless of how certified it all looked–Ole Debil works in strange ways. It never even crossed my consciousness that obviously the rules differed there. Rules were rules and no thank you, I'll just have bread and rice.

With time and luck, some of us have figured out that there are differences in rules as with everything else and we began to carry a little self-determination in making our distinctions. The post-ecumenical Church prepared the way for this loosening. If one is taught for twenty years that eating meat on Friday is a mortal sin, and then overnight it is no longer a mortal sin, one gets a little different perspective on things.

The Church has always taught that a mortal sin must have certain conditions present to actually qualify it as such–serious matter, adequate reflection, and full consent of the will–but somehow that narrow definition never had anything to do with the ''automatic'' mortal sins. In actuality, there can be no such thing as an automatic mortal sin, and no one but God and the person will ever know whether the required conditions were actually present–well, that's what the books said, but the teachers went right on tabulating the lists of automatic mortal sins, and few of their pupils saw any conflict between the two.

Until recently, advanced Catholic education rarely lessened this dissonance. One learned a few innocuous loopholes but, in the main, was still protected from oneself. Abortion was one area that was so instinctively heinous that it was rarely even spoken of. It was KILLING–MURDER–and as such needed no study to determine one's position on it.

The traditional Catholic argument against abortion has centered around the definition of the personal soul as being fully present from the moment of conception.* Therefore abortion at any stage of fetal development has been considered as murder.

*See note at end of section.

However this interpretation has not been consistent even within the Catholic tradition, for agreement could never be reached as to the precise time that human life began in the womb. Thomas Aquinas related the existence of the personal soul to the presence of the human body form in the developing fetus and defined the existence of the human soul as occurring four to six weeks after conception. Other theologians fixed the time of "life" at the first moment of "quickening"-*felt* life-which occurs somewhere in the fourth month of pregnancy.

The issue bobbed back and forth for centuries, remaining a thorn in the Church's flesh, until 1869, when Pius IX eliminated the distinction between the animated and non-animated fetus and proclaimed all abortions as murder. Some people maintain that his declaration was not motivated purely on spiritual grounds. They argue that the Church was ambitious to increase her fold and it was around this time that the development of birth control devices and their widespread usage began to threaten the Catholic population-and that this political consideration was bolstered by the Church' longstanding belief that sexual activity was only for purposes of procreation.

It is just as possible that the issue was brought to a head by the proclamation of the dogma of the Immaculate Conception, which occurred in 1854 by the same Pope. This dogma holds Mary, the mother of God, to have been conceived immaculate, i.e., free from original sin and thus a perfect vessel to bear Christ--differing from other babies who carry the stains of original sin until baptism. If Mary were *conceived* immaculate, that meant that her personal soul was present from the moment of conception and didn't come into existence at four weeks, six weeks, or at "quickening." To be consistent with this dogma, abortion at *any* time had to be simultaneously condemned.

Regardless of one's suspicions of the Church's past motivations, there is no doubt that abortion is a serious moral matter since it involves a decision that will bear on another's existence. Here lies the crux of the matter. What is the distinction between an "existence" and a "life?" Philosophical and medical distinctions abound, but none are conclusive. Certainly in conception, one is dealing with some form of life, but when does it become life as we recognize it?

Streptoccous culture in a dish has life. Ova and sperm are forms of life also--living things that have potentiality for continued viability given proper conditions--and this has been the basis of the Church's rationale against the use of contraception, which has been viewed as artificial interference with this potentiality. But the Church hasn't been entirely consistent even with this limited life form. If a woman aborts spontaneously, the moral matter is eliminated because of the lack of intention-- yet the aborted fetus is not accorded a burial nor baptized unless it has progressed to a recognizable human form. So even the Church herself seems to make some distinction as to when an existence becomes a real life.

Get beyond the problem of when existence becomes life, and greater problems lie in wait. Be convinced that it is life at any time–even agree that it becomes a matter of taking a life–murder–and the issue is still not clear-cut. Murder is an ugly word, but the Church has always recognized some acceptable varieties of it. She has allowed murder in wars, even to the extent of taking sides and providing chaplains to bless the "good" soldiers before they went out to kill; she has sanctioned it in capital punishment. Here, she doesn't even have the comforting ambiguity of whether life is present or not–war and capital punishment entail murdering *adults*–real persons at the height of their developmental powers. She has glided over this when pointing out her "justifiable" conditions. It gives me no slight problem to allow killing of grown people while giving no quarter for unviable fetuses.

Then there is the serious question of an individual's right and duty to decide her own moral questions. Basic to the Church herself is her dogma of "free will."

If a wartime killing can be justified on the grounds of the "greater good" this same rationale can also apply to a pregnant woman's decision about abortion. She can measure *her* life against another's; and if she is convinced that it is for the greater good of her life not to bear a child, she is making essentially the same distinction that the Church has made in wartime.

One must be consistent. If one holds the conviction that killing is never justified under any circumstances, that's quite a different matter. Some individuals hold that consistency personally, but the Church has never held it and can't play each decision by different rules, allowing killing in one case and condemning it in the next.

That why it's essential that individual moral decisions be taken out of Mother Church's willing hands. She can and should exist as a guide to help one make a well-considered decision, but in the end, one's life comes back to rest upon the individual. She is the one who will suffer any consequences if her decision has been wrong, so she is the only one who can and should make it.

Non-Catholics understandably chafe under the Catholic Church's determination to force her moral views on people who are not her members. Certainly, in many issues, an institution or an individual has a right–even an obligation–to tell truth as she sees it. Waging war is a good example of this. Perhaps once, one could find justifiable grounds for it; but today, none exist. I believe war is always wrong, nothing justifies engaging in it, and I invest a lot of energy in trying to impose this belief of mine on people who believe differently. In one sense, I would like to take away their freedom to hold a different value because I am convinced that theirs is wrong and mine is right. But I recognize that there are boundaries beyond which I cannot impose my belief. I cannot kill people who do not think my way. In the end I am limited to persuasion and example and commitment. This directly analogizes the Church's rigid position on abortion. To be true to herself, she must make every effort to convince people of what she considers the errors of their ways. She can marshal her resources to convince and persuade, but she cannot use those same resources to force and strip people of their final decision. Her money and power and good intentions are abused if she uses them as preventatives of free choice, rather than facilitators of dedicated sincere beliefs. The Church has been grievously wrong to ignore the war in Vietnam and spend millions of dollars trying to prevent people outside her faith from exercising their own "free will."

Morality is different for each person. No one can decide that theirs is better or more true. A believer in God in the end makes her vow with God, not to a church or state. An atheist is just as bound by his own perceived code of morality.

For many people today, population density is a real moral issue, not a side irrelevancy. They protest further births on the grounds that they will endanger lives already present. If one believes that unchecked propagation threatens the very basis of human life itself, let alone humanly liveable life, and favors limiting birth conducive to human dignity and freedom, abortion can be viewed as a real moral criterion. To deny the validity of this gets one back again to whose morality is better, and this is just what the Church must extricate herself from. Neither Heaven nor earth are provided just for Catholics.

Mother Church and many of her members feel threatened, but that is not rational. No one is going to force Catholics to have abortions against their will. If every country in the world legally allows abortions to occur, there is still no way a Catholic would have to undergo one against her will. Even many of the Catholics who decide to have them would not necessarily leave the Church if they were not driven out. There's paranoia here again, but it's not pure paranoia. It reeks a little too much of a perverted grasp for power and control. Catholics who condemn everyone else indiscriminately would do well to examine their own motives and consider again the autonomy of individual free will.

We don't live in a church-state. One must distinguish between what is legal and what is moral. A Catholic judge who takes his religion very seriously can grant a divorce to a couple with the certain knowledge that one or both will remarry. Divorce and remarriage are legal acts in this country, whatever one feels about their morality. When abortion becomes a law willed by a country's majority, one can accept the legality of it while maintaining her personal moral reservations and free choice.

There are other factors. Some people have no trouble with "justifiable" abortion, as in cases of women who are victims of rape or incest. Others of my staunchly traditional Catholic friends maintain that those circumstances are indeed unfortunate, but should be viewed as the will of God and possible paths to greater purification. They are consistently adamant, but I am no longer able to perceive the matter so spiritually. A child willed or desired by its parents has a better chance of human life. To force a child on a woman who does not want it is to limit its chances of a humanly worthwhile life and can have grievous consequences for the woman's life also.

Some people have no trouble with the moral implications of abortion but resist greatly the Movement's emphasis on *free* abortions. I understand this line of thinking least of all. It is a fact, that in this country, poor people get poor medical attention. Health is a basic right for all, but the only way poor people will ever receive it, is to make it free for everyone. I suspect that an insistence on *paying* for one's abortion disguises an element of paying more than money–it's a little too close to puritanical notions of punishment for wayward ways–"If you do such things, you should *pay* for them."

Monetary considerations aside, a great deal of the problem comes from viewing the whole issue of reproduction in a negative way. Instead of saying, "Thou Shalt Not Destroy," we should long ago have begun to say, "Thou Shalt Thoughtfully and Carefully Create."* The Church is reaping what she has sown in her appallingly blind insistence on procreation.

Abortion is a lousy form of contraception. It is a sad, sorry alternative to personal control of procreation. Hopefully, its very existence will become moot with the availability of safe, 100% reliable forms of family planning. Until that happens, we have to cope with unwanted progeny and the individual's right to determine her own destiny–without the consolation of a simple moral absolute–only a sliding scale of many interrelated values which must be seen in their interaction and judged in their particular context.*

***

*In the preparation of this chapter, background, fresh ideas, and an occasional phrasing were gratefully taken from articles previously written by Rosemary Reuther, Ida Kosciesza, and Carol Driscoll. My conclusions do not necessarily agree with theirs.

CHILDCARE CENTERS

"I always wanted babies. It's just that no one ever told me they'd turn into children."

Kids! When they're little, they fill their pants and pick their noses. Finally get them house-broken and they turn into shrieking banshees, picking a fight around every corner. They have an uncanny ability to take any innocuous circumstance and whomp it into a glorious, knock-down-drag-out confrontation. "Who got the yellow glass today?" "You *know* I only like peanut butter spread on half my bread!" Endure and you end up with teary adolescents who delight in embarrassing you with peculiar hair styles and ragtag clothes. I have long suspected that myopia plays a larger part than biology in determining that the young shall produce children. Young adults are the only ones rash and smug enough to even consider the immense task of child-rearing.

Just when one decides that a dog would be less trouble and more fun, children have some primeval survival mechanism that switches on and produces a wide-eyed lisped declaration of love. In the nick of time, your sensibilities get fuddled and clouded and one more chance is granted. Such are the tenuous crumbs that deflect infanticide, and parenthood bumbles on.

If being a parent is difficult, being a child is downright folly. It's really tough to be a kid. Subject to the commands and insults of anyone who is an inch taller or a month older, they have no power other than crude manipulation or wearing one down. Even these avenues can backlash as often as they work. Adults' vagaries determine their lives. Bigness is the automatic credential to wield power's reins and it's only available to the big.

Today's child has the further hindrance of living in a bizarre world of television and technology. We push them to live in this new world and get angry when they do. While we marvel that a five year old knows of rockets and atoms, we are unsympathetic when he can't amuse himself with simpler pursuits. "Whadda mean you don't have anything to do? Go out and stare at the sky. When *I* was a child . . ." and then comes the rhapsody of our own golden childhood hours spent in contemplating the mysteries of a blade of grass, until their eyes film over and they fidget to an escape. I'm skeptical of some of our bleary memories, but it seems that simple to us now.

There's no doubt that once life was simpler for everyone. Years ago, freedom was easier given. A child could get up early and wander around for miles, looking and learning and storing up secret childhood caches. He didn't have to keep an eye peeled for the friendly neighborhood pervert or cope with superhighway traffic.

Simpler times had simpler rules. Many of them were unfair and archaic, but they were *there*, unquestioned, bringing freedom by their very consistency. Parents didn't have their direction constantly confused by Spock, Genet, and Ginot–they were *the parents*! Their confidence might have been misplaced, but it was certain. Today instant media communication of the latest child research has us all bending over backwards to be fair and to be knowledgeable–usually it just ends up with our changing the rules every day, bringing bewilderment and inconsistency.

That's progress. It's a waste of time trying to hold onto a simpler era. Even whether the remembered era actually existed is moot–it doesn't exist now. It's time we faced the fact that circumstances have altered parents' needs and their progenies' as well. Our present provisions for dealing with children are hopelessly inadequate.

Americans have the added disadvantage of a cultural disinclination for children. We just are not big on kids. We marvel at the Italians who greet any child in a friendly, interested manner. "It's incredible," we say. "They like *all* children," thus revealing our own ambivalence. We are even able to grudgingly admire the ways Scandinavian countries have forged a healthy compromise between the demands of child-rearing and their parents' needs, but our ideology disallows the possibility of doing similarly. "That's all right for communists and socialists, but it'd never work for Americans."

Instead we delude ourselves that we are a "child-centered" society because we buy our children more toys per capita than any other nation on earth. Only in America could such a sick measure emerge. Shhh! about the reasons we buy our kids so many toys–the desperate hope for temporary pacifiers to keep them out of our way and out of our hair.

We don't readily welcome children anyplace either. All over invisible signs are posted that frown, "NO CHILDREN ALLOWED." Museums and galleries are ostensibly open to all ages, but just let a child act like a child and quicken her step or raise her voice and censure immediately descends. Though many of us are hesitant to confront rude or loud adults, our propriety knows no such restraint when the matter involves children. We hasten to tell one and all just where children do and do not belong.

Rarely does anyone have a Sunday afternoon party with children warmly included. We leave them home with the babysitter, barely able to keep from running down the sidewalk–"for God's sake, we need a little time to ourselves." We never admit to any of these practices because one of the marks of a civilization is how it treats its young, and we like to fancy ourselves a civilized people.

We are *often* put upon by our children, but we've brought it upon ourselves by our reluctance to consider them as a normal part of community life–by not allowing them to be around us and model their behavior on the adults. We keep them away from the "civilized" members of the society, i.e., *us*, and then bemoan their savageness. While we know that children are the most valuable resource of any society–indeed are the insurance and perpetuation of the society itself–we don't like to assign any collective responsibility for them. We shy away from communal responsibility even in unstructured situations. Show me the parent who'll treat a neighbor's child as his own and I'll show you a dumb parent or a nineteenth century remnant. Americans are independent critters–it's one of our God-given rights–and don't mess with it, Buddy.

Nothing would be wrong with any of this if it worked. It doesn't work. We end up with bothersome children and weary and frustrated adults. Instead of facing up to the lacks of our present day solutions, we keep kidding ourselves that we are bound by the status quo–we resign ourselves to a pitiful dependence upon time to alleviate our problem. It's quite true that no child lasts longer than twenty years, but that's not the most sensible use of two decades. Why not combine a little realistic romanticism–that children can and should be a glorious experience–with a little of the good old American know-how of efficiently handling production problems? One way that has the potential of doing this is the providing of childcare centers.

Talk of childcare centers weaves in and out of periods, welling different emotions each time. Currently, it's throwing people into a tizzy, raising outlandish accusations. The curious thing is that for the first time, present day demands are motivated on human grounds as opposed to previous motivations based on economic crisis.

Historically when childcare centers have been set up, it was to meet economic stress, as during the Depression and World War II, when women were needed for the labor force. Focus was on facilitating production–when the crisis disappeared, so did the childcare centers. Americans have never had much difficulty with the gross national product mentality; it's when the focus changes to purely human needs that the purists start their outcries.

Childcare centers are not the big deal that people are trying to make them out to be. For those who want to keep the women down on the farm, they do fulfill the requirements of a commie plot–they'll undermine the family and take momma away and have the government butting in again where it doesn't belong. But the paranoiacs have to fudge a few facts to maintain their fears. In the U.S. today there are thirty-two million working women[1] who have left the farm and are not going back. Their children under the age of six total almost six million.[2] 1.8 million of the families listed as "poor" in America are headed by women, who *must* work to buy bread, or depend on welfare.[3] Many other women have an economic or personal need to work and their numbers increase daily. You can talk yourself blue in the face about where they *belong*, but women are not staying in the home for a variety of reasons.

Childcare centers can no longer be considered a "necessary evil" for the poor; they have become an essential need of all sectors of society. They aren't an answer to the *women's* problem either; they are a *people's* liberation issue. There's nothing noble about "key children," the little kids who wear an apartment key strung round their necks, to enable them to open their doors and wait alone inside until a parent gets off her shift. Even romantics can't pretend that a series of transient "housekeepers" can maintain a Louisa May Alcott home without effects being visited upon the whole family.

---

[1] Woman's Bureau, Department of Labor, July, 1971.

[2] U.S. Department of Labor, publication 71-283, May, 1971.

[3] Robert Stein, "The Economic Status of Families Headed by Women," *Monthly Labor Review*, December, 1970.

Today, finding adequate childcare is not a question of money. Even people who have adequate financial resources at their disposal can rarely find "ideal" solutions. Ironically, that's what's bringing the issue to a head–the middle class is feeling the pinch. When only "poor" people had to put up with inadequate solutions and provisions, well that was a damned shame, but one couldn't expect them to lead optimum lives. When the man making twenty thousand dollars a year has a wife who wants to work, and *they* can't find adequate childcare, the oppression takes on a different meaning. The middle class has picked up the childcare banner because it's now in our best interests to do so.

There are private childcare centers existing today. Many of them have been irretrievably warped by the profit motive, running on rigid schedules, following mass production rules, and bound to show an annual profit to justify their existence. They perpetuate the same evils of the public school system–emphasizing passivity, programming, and blind obedience–with a lamentable head start on younger minds. They are not any solution.

In the vanguard of the childcare center press is the Women's Movement. Because a lot of people are threatened by "those women," the issue has become clouded with irrelevancies. Opponents are responding to what they *think* advocates are asking for, not to what is really asked. Because the demand takes the form of "twenty-four hour childcare centers," it is automatically assumed that we advocate dumping our children for twenty-four hour periods. No one desires this. Round-the-clock centers are demanded because they must be available to meet the needs of all. An eight-to-five center will not help the parent who works at night, or on a split shift.

People fantasize every conceivable abuse to avoid realistic appraisals of providing daycare centers. They are far less complicated than our public school system but the mechanics of that don't heat the emotions or seem insurmountable. Either it's more socially acceptable to foist off one's children for seven hours a day at the magical age of six, or we're more tired out by then.

For the record, what is a childcare center? It is a place especially provided for children–that exists, welcomes, and is equipped for them. A place that through a combination of money, space, effort, and love can provide an environment in which they can thrive and develop, grow and have fun.

The money and space for it can be borne by either government or institutions or a combination of both–on the *sole* grounds that children are a prime vital resource. Absolutely no consideration of it as a facilitator of increased profit or production should be allowed, although this may be one of its side benefits. Community members should retain control of it to ensure that its values do not get muddied or confused. In our public schools we've relinquished the control, and there's no reason to repeat the same mistake.

It should be staffed by people who *like* children and are trained and inclined to nurture them. By training, I do not necessarily mean professional pedigree. There are plenty of certified teachers and child experts who do not like kids. Some training of the craft of child-rearing should be expected and required, but in the end, there's an art to it that is not given to all equally.

It should have equipment scaled to child size and needs, as finances permit. It there is a temporary lag between actualization of centers and acceptance of responsibility by government and institutions, imagination and invention can surmount temporary lacks.

The books, media, and toys in it should be asexual and aracial. Attitudes toward sex, race, work, and oneself form early–they should be recognized and reckoned with early. In most cases, this means that new books will have to be written and new toys will have to be demanded and produced. The bulk of existing materials perpetuate blatant sexist stereotypes. Primers show Daddy going off to work while Mommy stays home cleaning the house. Boys' toys reflect *activity*–chemistry sets, doctor's kits, erector sets (Man The Builder). Girls' toys reflect *service*–pint-size housecleaning tools, dolls, nurse's kits. Popular career games show the same restrictions. Girls can spin the wheel and become: a model (What a figure!), stewardess (What a figure!), secretary, dental hygienist, nurse (Woman The Consoler). Boys spin and become: an astronaut, executive, dentist, doctor. It is no accident that the wheel of fortune has the girls' and boys' choices insidiously complementing each other.

Many advocates view childcare centers as a cooperative community venture. Ideally it should be cooperative in a truly altruistic sense–one puts in what one can and takes out what one needs. Some will be able to contribute greater physical and psychological gifts, others more money and time, but it should not be limited to what and when one can give. As a community resource and responsibility, the functioning of it should not be dependent upon the goodwill of individual parents.

Any serious attempt at making childcare centers cooperative ventures is going to depend upon a radical transformation in our attitudes toward children and child-rearing. Emotionally we will have to view and accept children as normal, natural parts of our community whole. Professionally, we must begin to regard child-rearing as a skilled, delicate occupation and utilize existing knowledge and techniques to foster proper and whole development.

It is pure folly to continue pretending that child-rearing comes naturally. (Sixty thousand children are battered, burned, maimed, and killed annually by parents it didn't come naturally to.) Child-raising, like all human interactions, demands effort, takes skill, and requires experience and training.

We're funny about that in America. We pay great glory to college degrees and insist that all professions meet measurable standards, with the glaring exception of child-rearing. We commit a grievous error by trying to push every woman to produce and raise children, regardless of her personal desires or inclinations. Then we compound our error by considering the whole process immune from training. Mere biology gets one into it, and often hope and luck are the only things that get one through it.

It is not realistic to expect a person who has never been around children to automatically surge with love and delight toward them. Instead of recognizing this as a natural reaction to a new situation, we put a stigma on such feelings, adding guilt to a person who is already bumbling and inadequate. Everyone is supposed to like children–"What are you, some kind of pervert? You probably don't even like dogs." Every other profession automatically presupposes training, and yet in the most sensitive profession of all, we blithely ignore the whole matter.

Visualize a childcare center run as an altruistic, cooperative effort, requiring participation from all community members–married, single, divorced, widowed, youngsters, oldsters, and middlings. Some of these will have a natural gift for child-rearing, the same way some people have a flair in all their human interactions. Others will have discovered many good routes through previous trial and error–still another segment will be knowledgeable in the latest findings in child research. Combine these strengths and make them available to the remaining participants who do not presently possess them. Get rid of the emotional stigma and approach the whole business like any other new job. If a bricklayer were using Elmer's glue, it would be pointed out to him quickly enough. Be as realistic in the infinitely more precarious task of socializing another human being.

Since everyone would be required to give some effort to raising society's children—again on the sole grounds that they are the insurance of the society itself—the commitment would be automatic, leaving only the skills to be acquired. With a massive effort, this could come in time to save many of those parents who detest child-rearing and yet have children. One's enjoyment in a job is certainly influenced greatly by one's competence at it. People who have stumbled into parenthood for the wrong reasons—societal pressures or expectations—might come out of it with the right reasons. Adolescents would have the opportunity, exposure, and experience upon which to more rationally base their own future reproductive decisions.

If we aren't going to attempt this transformation in emotional and professional attitudes, then it would be better to keep the discontented parents away from direct contact with the children. They could contribute money, maintenance, bookkeeping, etc., to fulfill their societal obligation.

For most people, a childcare center is justified simply as a practical means to handle the problems of childcare, but many of its advocates also have a strong ideology for it. Different individuals view it:

–as a means to enable women to stop exploiting other women–a desirable alternative to the sorry practice of underpaying a needy woman to take care of one's kids.

–as an end to the constant turnover of transient, often ill-equipped teenage babysitters, most of whom are at best only a body stopgap to grant a temporary reprieve.

–as a potential opportunity to broaden children's development–to have them experience direct exposure to many adults, not restricted to the limitations of one's particular set of biological parents.

–as making a commitment to their children.*

---

*Cooperative nursery school mothers have long experienced the phenomenon of finding that the weekly required participation becomes pleasurable rather than endured duty. It's simply because one has accepted the commitment to completely give of herself for a specified time, as opposed to the same block of time at home where housework and other responsibilities interfere, resulting in begrudged time.

There are few "fulltime" mothers who say, "Today I will spend three hours with my child." Even when exterior demands don't interfere, it is tremendously difficult to devote large blocks of quality time to a child. Read a story, share a glass of kool-ade, paint a picture, and the unbelieving eye sees that the clock has passed a half-hour. Even sincere attempts often end

–as a chance to break possessive feelings they hold for their children. By sharing the responsibility, they hope to stop regarding their own child as a personal possession reflecting upon their worth and subject to their vagaries.

–as a facilitator of increased community–with all members working together for common goals–with children viewed as a normal part of that community life with shared responsibility and pleasures flowing to all.

–Freudian-oriented parents see it as an opportunity to lessen the Oedipal conflict in small children. With more adults around, possible conflict arising from the typical nuclear situation is dispersed.

The large majority of people advocating child-care centers may share some of these reasons or all of them. But most motives are not clear-cut. Generally it boils down to the parent having experienced frustrations in trying to maintain the burdens and pressures alone and simply wishing to dilute them by sharing. This is certainly a valid reason and much more sensible than sticking with the unsatisfactory setting, ending up weary and cranky and taking it out on one's kids.

up with many "fulltime" mothers merely offering their physical bodies for their child's contemplation, while shutting them out in much more subtle ways.

In a setting provided for children with other children and adults, time can flow easier.

Most of the objections to childcare centers arise from fears of possible abuse of the mechanics of the system, not the system itself. The most vociferous accusation is that childcare centers will become dumping grounds. There's no doubt that when these facilities become widely available, some parents will race breakneck to dump their kids. All the more reason to have such places. Though unfortunate, it's true that many people today are reluctant parents. It's infinitely more healthy for their progeny to be "dumped" into an environment that welcomes them, rather than to stay in an unwanted setting twenty-four hours a day. At the very least, it will provide a temporary respite from their parents' frustrations and regrets–give them a chance to be around adults who do like children and are willing to devote time to them–and provide them with models more oriented to accept children.

Another fear is that the system will become rigid, ending up as the "other place" besides home for children to go. To be either at the center or at home is no great liberation. Two places are not enough stimuli for a developing child. Even a child at home is not limited to two choices–her mother will take her to the park one day, the store the next, a concert on the third. This possible "blunting" could be avoided by having an abundance of centers, one in each community, with a child able to "float" between different ones. Very young children–some older children–will need stability of setting at different periods, and this obviously must be taken into consideration. But most children, given the opportunity and freedom, are able to adjust quite easily and with joy to new environments. Since the centers would be staffed by a variety of adults, it is to be supposed that various ones would take on the unique characteristics of their participants. One might excel in physical education, another have a flair for art projects. A child able to float between neighborhood community centers could reap the benefits of each, according to his desires and capacities of the time. Centers also should be "open" from city to city. A visit to grandma would not have to be an exhausting experience–when grandma was tired, the child could become a "visiting guest" at her neighborhood center.

Concern about a child's need for stability emerges in other areas also. For this reason, each center should contain a permanent staff–not *one* teacher, for this only fosters a new limited dependence and allegiance–but a team comprised of a combination of men and women. They would always be there–permanent fixtures to bring a sense of permanence to a child. The staff could then draw upon interested volunteers–community resources to enrich the basic environment. Mr. Jones the carpenter could come in and help the four year olds learn to handle basic tools–Mrs. Ghandi from India could tell of her country and explain the intricacies of wrapping a sari and tying a turban.

One unexpected valuable resource that has emerged in childcare centers being tried today are the many single people who have willingly offered their help. Though not wishing full commitment to children, they still desire contact with them. It continues to amaze weary parents, but it is not an infrequent occurrence and should be welcomed and utilized.

One must be careful to draw a fine line between having enough adults to provide plentiful attention without inundating the children. It might seem ideal to have the smallest ratio possible so that an adult could take two children off to a park if desired—another could have a quiet story with only one, etc. But too many adults can end up overwhelming the children and can also be a source of conflict between many people having to work within close quarters. This is a decision that will have to be played by ear, and numbers may have to be increased or decreased as the needs warrant.

Other possible problems are tied in with finances and can be resolved by such. Space is essential, proper equipment is important and money can buy these things.

None of the bugaboos people fear have to arise. None are intrinsic to the childcare concept itself. With time, dedication, and money, all can be avoided, ending up with a human solution to a human need.

Actually it's difficult to charge one's adrenalin up over the issue of childcare centers. The writing is so clearly on the wall. Even the President, a man equalled in reckless abandon only by Warren G. Harding, is saying the word right out loud in public.* When the politicians see political expediency in an issue, it's all over except for a little final hemorrhaging from the bleeding hearts. All that really remains now is to retain firm control and direction of their actualization. And to sit back in years to come and listen to one's grown children tell new little children of happy golden times spent in childcare centers–staring at the sky.

***

*My optimism was premature. The President, by vetoing the childcare bill recently passed by Congress, did indeed demonstrate reckless abandon–abandoning the urgent need of children. Again, the issue became clouded by political irrelevancies.

EQUAL PAY FOR EQUAL WORK

My great aunt Maud, in Indiana, doesn't give a hoot for most of my "liberation notions." "BALDERDASH!" is her frequently offered, unsolicited opinion. I've been tempted to retort that "BALLS!" comes closer to the mark, but she'd wash my mouth out with soap. She is a remarkable woman–true pioneer vintage–with a maddening talent for simplifying the most complicated issues. On overpopulation: "Floods and famine'll take care of a whole bunch of 'em. The Good Lord'll provide for the rest."

Childcare centers are dispensed with even quicker–"Children belong in the home–they're let out in public far too early these days." Having raised eight children single-handed–without one murderer in the bunch–she speaks with a straight tongue and an unconfused heart.

But switch the topic to "equal pay for equal work" and she's practically grabbing your picket sign to race you to the nearest rally. As she puts it, "Work is work, and them that does, gets."

Aunt Maud's got it clear enough on that one. It's just about that simple except for the minor fact that that's not the way it is. Women are grossly underpaid whether they are doing "women's" work or "men's" work. They are consistently denied equal opportunity regardless of their qualifications, on the sole basis of sex.

Caroline Bird, The Equal Employment Opportunity Commission, The Women's Bureau of the Labor Department can all provide statistics that will make your blood boil, but here's a few quick verbal karate chops to use the next time you meet a caveman who wonders what all the hullabaloo's about.

"She'll only get married and have children and drop out of the labor force anyway!"

1. One-tenth of *all* women remain single.[1]

1a. One-tenth of *all* married women do not have children.[2]

[1]Marijean Suelzle, "Women in Labor," *Transaction*, Nov.-Dec., 1970.
[2]*Ibid.*

"A woman ought to stay home and take care of her children."

    2. The average mother will have approximately forty years or *one-half* of her life ahead of her, after her youngest child is in school.[3]

On "equal" opportunity:

    3. 37% of the entire labor force are women but they hold 70% of all clerical positions, 99% of domestic employment, and 59% of all service work.[4]

    3a. One-third of all working women are employed in seven occupations–secretary, saleswoman, elementary schoolteacher, domestic, bookkeeper, waitress, and nurse.[5]

On women's work as being "pin money pastime:"

    4. 5.6 million families are headed by a woman.[6]

    4a. 1.8 million families classified as "poor" have a female head who is the sole breadwinner.[7]

[3]*Ibid.*

[4]Joreen, "The 51% Minority Group: A Statistical Essay," in *Sisterhood Is Powerful*, edited by Robin Morgan, 1970.

[5]*The 1969 Handbook on Women Workers*, Women's Bureau, No. 294, U.S. Department of Labor.

[6]Robert Stein, "The Economic Status of Families Headed by Women," *Monthly Labor Review,* Dec., 1970.

[7]*Ibid.*

On who's really discriminated against:

    5. Median wages descend in this order–white men, black men, white women, black women.[8]

    6. The median income of women who have completed five or more years of college is $9,262; men with identical educational background earn $13,788.[9]

One can find a variety of reasons that "justify" these conditions. No small part of the problem comes from women themselves who have readily accepted them. Weak self-concepts nurtured by educational brainwashing–culturally sexist stereotypes confining both men and women to restricted patterns of behavior and response–and an economy's insatiety for ever-spiraling profits–have birthed and perpetuated them. But the times they are a changin'.

1969 Handbook on Women Workers, Department of Labor, Table 61, p. 137.

"Fact Sheet on the Earnings Gap," U.S. Department of Labor, Feb., 1971.

CHAPTER 6

ONE MAN'S FAMILY

ONE MAN'S FAMILY

G. "You know, Roger, every time we solve one thing, it just seems to reveal another problem underneath."

R. "Oh I don't know. I think we've come pretty far in the last year."

G. "But so many problems seem to lie *outside* of us. Like I've been thinking a lot about the nuclear family lately."

***

"Your husband really must be nice. Whenever you talk about him, he sounds so kind and giving."

"He is. He's just perfect, except for two things. He believes in monogamy and the nuclear family."

America is a nation of the present. We have no past, no history, only a collection of myths that have persisted because of their romantic appeal or

138

exploitative value. George Washington would not tell a lie about cutting down the cherry tree– Lincoln walked ten miles to return a penny. Females were faithful wives and super-giving nurses. Negroes were contented darkies or uppity Reconstructionists. The Wild West frontier tradition gives Americans an intrinsic right to bear arms.

We pride ourselves on being a "Now" people.* Those who are not "with it" now are obsolete and of no value to us. Our disdain of indirect experience shows in our treatment of our old people. We kick them out of their jobs and shut them away in institutions with paid keepers. We segregate them in "senior citizen havens" with their own kind, efficiently quieting many simultaneously. We shuffle them around from relative to relative until their prattling of the past and their ways become intolerable. As a civilization, we fare poorly in our treatment of our old, but we continue to close them out because their reminiscences interfere with our present perceptions.

*It might be argued that we are actually a nation of the future, because we are so future-oriented in our "success ethic." In our personal lives, we do often defer today's pleasures to tomorrow's rewards–shape our present behavior to insure future benefits. We encourage children to strive for grades that will enable them to get into college, rather than learning for its own sake. We readily assume the burdens of large mortgages and debts that will result in future ownership. Young men work inordinate hours during their "peak

Exclusion of the past may facilitate the present, but it doesn't aid one to form a different future. One cannot profit from past mistakes or successes if one is unaware of them. Most of our young do not know that our country now faces many problems that have been faced before. Most things are not falsified deliberately–they are simply obliterated or overlooked. Lives are determined by all kinds of patterns that have only existed a short time.

Being an adolescent of the fifties, I was particularly shaped by silence. In the aftermath of the McCarthy terror, I never heard anything questioned because my mentors were still too frightened by what had happened to previous inquisitiveness. McCarthy, himself, was only a vague name to me.

My "higher" education took place in quiet also. For four years, I lived in a gentle ghetto, a Catholic girls' college, which concentrated on training young girls to become old girls. I loved it.

performance" years to amass financial success for their later years.

But these postponements are still geared toward perpetuating a future that is the same as our present "now." We make certain compromises because we automatically assume that the status quo will remain unchanged. On a much larger scale, we show our disconcern with shaping a different future by allowing pollution to continue rampant, scorning city-planning and continuing to erect eye-sore environments for temporary gains–by simply not considering the possibility that our future may evolve in quite different directions.

The rules were rigid and archaic–laughable to today's youth. Until I was a senior, smoking on campus meant automatic expulsion. Lights were turned out at 10:00 each night–a growing girl needs her sleep. I embraced the restrictions eagerly as evidence that someone cared enough to protect me.

We dressed formally for dinner–learned to gracefully balance teacups on our laps and minute philosophical distinctions in our heads. We only made distinctions among Catholic philosophers.

I took my degree in psychology, a risky field, but with careful guidance, we managed to skirt Freud in several days, tsk, tsking about his preoccupation with sex–the man was obsessed. That threat dispelled, we were able to study T.V. Moore in depth, a qualified if somewhat obscure psychologist. If the cynics maintained that one of Moore's virtues lay in his having kept the true religion, it only proved that our priorities were correct.

We prayed a lot too. And formed social consciences. Though I never heard of the goings-on in Alabama,* I did spend hours packing baskets to be distributed to the needy at holiday time. Not that we were Madame Bountifuls–if our solutions were short-sighted, our instincts were genuine.

*Martin Luther King was not exactly a name to inspire confidence in a Catholic heart.

We had one Negro in the school. Don't get the idea that she was a token, for all people are humans and brothers. She just never had a roommate because she was more comfortable that way.

One of the most valuable things I learned at my college was what constituted a "real" woman. That kind of knowledge is hard to come by these days.

This school and many like it no longer exist. My particular one is still putting out death rattles, trying desperately to "adjust" to the times and become "relevant," but demise is imminent. If its quest for relevancy is motivated by a lack of applications and a paucity of alumnae financial support, well, none of us are as purist as before.

My alma mater, like everything else, was a product of its times, mirroring the broader society around us. Though I frequently wonder, "Why me, God?" I temper my bitterness with this realization. I just happened to grow up when America was standing still.

All over, females were being subtly molded to fit into a post-war economy. During the war, women had performed every type of occupation. When the men returned, it was necessary to reduce the women to surplus to provide enough places. The women were only too willing to retreat into the tight private unit of the home and celebrate the survival of their men. Great mystique grew around the home and the homemaker. The role of wife-mother became glorified, with emphasis shifting from developing oneself as an individual identity to learning to perform a role. I really warmed to the Madonna image and was raring to climb up on my suttee.

Throughout my sixteen years of formal education, I was taught only what people wanted me to know. Enforced military conscription was the patriotic duty of a young man; no one mentioned that this only became law in the 1940's amidst tremendous resistance–that "draft-dodgers" were not a new phenomenon even then. Questioning one's government was tantamount to sacrilege; the protesting veterans, who were fired upon in the streets of Washington two decades ago, were not in my history books. Bloody labor riots, the mass killings in Boston during the Irish uprisings, also escaped my eyes. Especially good jokes were the fiercely dedicated feminists who risked life and security to obtain human rights. Abigail Adams was a shadowy, dutiful wife, with a demure gown in the Smithsonian–not a pained, raging woman, who threatened John with a "revolution if women were not considered but continued to be subjected to tyranny."

While my education protected me with censorship, my religion treated me as a diabetic one week and a mental defective the next. If I had ever wanted to taste exotic fruits–and I was never even tempted–pain of sin was an effective deterrent. Today women agonize over whether they have the right to decide when to bear children; silence shrouds the fact that theologians have disagreed for centuries over the exact moment that life becomes present–that abortion was only canonically declared as against God's "natural law" one hundred years ago.

Silent times, omission, and a religion zealous of its power, molded me well. I was a quick learner, and I modeled my aspirations and expectations on what I saw around me, on what was allowed to slip through my censors. One of my "dogmas" was the nuclear family.

The nuclear family is a unit of living, consisting of mother, father, and children. It is the base of our society and our economy. In our culture, it is synonomous with civilization. Until the advent of "hippies", few of our members ever experimented voluntarily or honestly with alternative ways of living.

The concept of nuclear families developed historically to meet the needs of the times. It had valid reasons for beginning, a rich tradition sustains it, and for many, it will have valid reasons for continuing. Neither paragon nor culprit, it is merely one mode of living, potentially good for some people, not good for others. The problems come when it is held up as the model way of living, the only correct route to contentment. We recognize that many other peoples have lived in different manners. Without a twinge to our egalitarian pretensions we have subtly implied that their ways are "primitive," distinguishing them from civilized peoples, i.e., *us*.

Many Western people today, through a combination of circumstances, do not live in a strictly defined nuclear setting. Divorced, widowed, and single people live differently, with and without children. Some "nuclear" families are really extended families, encompassing one or a set of grandparents. But most lacks that emerge in these other modes of living continue to be attributed to the deviance from the "norm," rarely judged as possible lacks in themselves. Simply because other ways of living sometimes produce dissatisfaction or unhappiness does not mean that the ways themselves are wrong–they may be sabotaged by our insistence on a single standard.

If a domineering mother-in-law moves in with her children, creating dissension and conflict, it does not follow that an extended family will not work in our culture or that their problems would be resolved by reverting to a strict nuclear family. Tensions introduced by the mother-in-law's presence may appear to prove the theory that "two's company and three's a crowd," but really, she may be a victim of that theory. She may feel herself an intruder–indeed in this setting, she *is* an intruder–may realize that she has little power or self-determination but must adjust within set confines. Possibly her carping and divisive ways come from a setting that cannot permit her to be accepted as an individual with unique things to contribute.

Similarly, a divorced woman may find her life-style unfulfilling and frustrating because she is trying to "make the best of a bad thing." The things that combine to make it unsatisfying–loneliness, unshared financial responsibility, restrictive sexual mores–can be the problems, not her way of life itself. If she must gear her social life to look for a mate to share her burdens rather than seek experiences that might enrich and fulfill her as an individual and refuse her natural sexual needs so as not to jeopardize her potentiality as a desireable spouse, then her life-style has small chance of being satisfying. In effect she must write off her way of life as something to be temporarily endured, until hopefully the "ideal" comes her way again. This is the real danger in holding one style of life as a model–alternative ways are not given fair testing.

It is entirely possible that Western civilization is too populous, too diverse, to expect all of its members to live in one way. One model is not available to all–to continue to hold it out and measure all other ways by it will only prevent them from fairly judging the potentialities of what is available. Many people will be lost before they can begin.

All people harbor interior isolation inside their secret places. We do many kinds of things to fill or obscure it, from religion to unceasing activity. Most of us are unaware that much of today's way of living systematically perpetuates our isolation.

First we isolate ourselves inside our families, with our families. We then proceed to extend this isolation by segregating people on every level. Some people segregate others by binding together only with those of similar nationality, color, religion, profession, economic status, neighborhood.

Almost all of us segregate people by age. We start this early. Three year olds invite only other three year olds to their birthday parties, usually of the same sex. Teenagers group together–young marrieds go with young marrieds–and old folks go into their peculiar communities. Except for weddings and funerals, the ages rarely mix. Look around at your next party. The widest span allowed occurs between ages thirty and fifty. Before and after this, the age range is much more tightly controlled. Even the maximum, twenty years, is curiously restricted when one considers that community members span seventy years plus.

Each age group is given a limited culture. Children are actively kept from "adult" things–surfeited with toys and ever-changing, often ill-equipped babysitters so that the grown-ups can go with their own kind, unhindered. Teenagers hang in some nether world, too old for childish things, but not yet welcomed as functioning, valuable adults. With the advent of their financial exploitability, they were provided with their own culture. There are clubs for young singles, mature singles, parents without partners, senior citizens. Our country is a giant phalanx of cliques and clans with everyone eligible for some limited place and membership, but the idea of mixing all ages affects people like incest.

Everyone guards his own weaknesses and is prevented from contributing his strengths across strictly defined boundaries. The results of this show most clearly in people's inability to communicate with each other. "I can't talk to my children." "I can't talk to my parents." "I can't talk to..."

On my street, by chance, there are some "old" people left. In the normal suburban neighborhood, they would long ago have been moved out. They rattle around in houses that are too big for them, existing quite inefficiently. These are the only neighbors who unreservedly welcome my children into their homes and affections. Their own children are grown and gone, removing them from the daily strains of child-rearing, and they now have time and inclination for little people. They give something valuable to my children and receive something of value in return.

A Cuban family lived here briefly, several families actually, sharing one house, until the landlord became wise to their violation of the suburban ethic of private dwellings. In this house, strange wonderful things went on as a matter of course. At a birthday party for their four year old, every child on the block was invited, ranging from nine months to eleven years. It was an impossible situation and they all had a marvelous time, staying five hours, having a many course dinner and general bedlam. The house was stuffed with adults so care and attention were plentiful. On ordinary days, their home was only slightly less attractive. A child could be warmly welcomed there and enjoyed for hours on end. These people might have gone on, bringing health and vitality from their culture to ours, but they made the mistake of raising chickens in their back yard. No one could expect a suburb like ours to assimilate mangy back yard poultry and a rooster who kept rooster's hours. When we speak of "gracious country living," we don't mean that kind of country. Before you could say, "Adios amigo," the Cubans took their chickens and open boisterous ways and disappeared from our lives.

I never thought I'd be waving a flag for old folks and foreign families with chickens. These possibilities were not part of my education or expectations. I was automatically programmed into seeking to establish a nuclear family unit–carefully trained not only to accept isolation, but to actively foster it. I expected and yearned to find one mate for life and raise a close-knit family. Together we would form an independent oasis, united in goal, impregnable from assault. The Kennedy dynasty would have nothing on me. I was enthusiastic about turning all my affections, talents, and energies toward my particular spouse and offspring.

This way of living may have benefits to recommend it, but its intrinsic characteristic of encouraging isolation is not one of them. Perhaps I never questioned it before because it fits in with our American notions of independence and individualism. We think that privacy will free us from the demands of others, but it can just as easily confine and restrict us, entrapping us in loneliness and aloneness. Guarding and maintaining one's privacy and private space can easily obscure the fact that many people share similar problems and burdens and that a binding together might produce an easier, quicker resolution of them. With our affections trained on a specific few, we rarely consider the possibility of affection and energy devoted to a larger community.*

Since good things can happen within the nuclear family–emotional bonds, sharing, laughter and joys–we are reluctant to consider living in other ways, for fear that we will lose the good things. Isolation inside a family with a family is infinitely better than isolation alone.

To try another way of living does not mean that one would automatically forfeit the benefits enjoyed in a family. The benefits may be entirely independent, thriving by themselves regardless of the particular setting. Why cannot one take the good things of their lives, weed out the unsatisfying things, and transplant the useful things into a potentially more satisfying surrounding?

Many people are beginning to question the rationale of the nuclear family. For some, it is based on neurotic dependencies rather than healthy emotional relationships, bringing sickness instead of soundness. For almost everyone, it is a confine within which it becomes increasingly difficult to raise unscarred children. It has too many pressures inherent in it. Any unhappiness or frustrations of its adult members are visited upon the unwitting children.

*Linda Gordon, "Functions of the Family," *Women: A Journal of Liberation*, Fall, 1969.

Part of this has resulted from the changing role of women. In pre-industrial times, today's particular tensions were not present. The family was the center of production with the woman holding a significant and functional role within it. Everything was produced in the home. Today women do not have to make bread, clothes, *anything* for the family members. Industrialization and specialization have reduced our functions to providing janitorial services, child-rearing, and filling psychological needs, which in many instances are caused by the family structure itself. Many women are in the bizarre position of relieving tensions while simultaneously creating them.

Even the special biological function of women is limited today. Formerly, large families were necessary and desirable to make more hands to lessen the work. Infant mortality was high, life expectancy low, and women spent many years birthing children. Advances in medicine and technology have rendered bumper crops of children unnecessary.

For the first time in history, we have the phenomenon where many women have to devote themselves to being full-time mothers in order to have enough to do. Trying to fill up a life by living through others' lives has become synonomous with feminine fulfillment.

Generally the mother is totally responsible for filling all emotional and physical needs of her children. If she is tired or cranky, their needs must go unmet. If she happens to be neurotic or frustrated, their chance for sound emotional lives is diminished accordingly. Since the mother obtains most of her self-worth from how well the family functions, everything personally reflects upon her. If the house is not clean, the children not well-behaved and properly groomed, her husband not succored, the unit is lessened and she bears the bulk of failure.

The father is burdened by being the sole financial support of the family. Whether he is able to fulfill this function or not, it remains the cultural expectation. In the many cases where the mother must work to supplement his earnings, we pretend that this is not the reason. We dismiss her working as "pin money" pastime–say it is only a means to procure extras and luxuries–even when the "luxuries" have become necessities because of our standard and pace of living. The mother *needs* a vacuum cleaner and washing machine, or her ability to perform her part well is interfered with. They all *need* a vacation–a change of scene–a television–to refresh themselves (or escape temporarily) in order to go back and cope with the problems of maintaining the unit again. Since our society does not psychologically allow couples to jointly assume financial responsibility for the family, a woman may feel resentment or scorn toward her husband when he is unable to maintain the financial burdens alone. A man may feel personal failure for his inability to perform his "masculine role" and "provider." Even when the psychological pressures are absent, most men must sacrifice the bulk of their time with their families and shared family pleasures to fulfill their financial obligations.

While the father is expected to pay for the maintaining of the unit, and the mother must keep the atmosphere and provide the environment so that the unit can thrive, in many cases, the children have been reduced to the personal possessions of the unit. Though their physical contributions are no longer necessary, we have evolved a situation where their psychological services are often greatly in need. Children are used to assuage parental frustrations–to bring glory to the family name–to be what their parents could not be. Their behavior, their very lives, reflect upon their parents.

To ensure the efficiency of the unit, individuality can be tolerated only within strictly defined limits. The children bear most of the brunt of adjusting, because they have the least power in the family. We say routinely, "Joe's room is cleaner than yours." or "I never have this problem with Mary. What's the matter with you?" These needling remarks may help to get things accomplished, but they don't bear close examination. So what if Joe's room is cleaner than Sue's? What does that have to do with Sue? Perhaps Joe can only thrive in a neat environment–maybe order is not so important or necessary to Sue. But efficiency is necessary to the functioning of the family, so we produce a common denominator everyone must adjust to. If in the adjustment, individual growth and choice must be thwarted, that is the price one pays for membership.

I do not advocate total freedom or lack of authority for my children. But I grieve when I must bend their reaching out for self-determination to my insecurities and frustrations. When they encroach on my *authority*, it is not just authority when I retort, "Do it because *I* said to do it." This is despotism. When I fear that they will reflect poorly on me as a "good mother," I am burdening them with my "needs"–showing my dependence upon them to make me worthwhile, a success.

In the attempt to maintain our affluent life-style, I must force children to do vast amounts of useless housework–to care for possessions that bring little pleasure. I pretend that it teaches them responsibility, but don't kid yourself. A five year old scrubbing toilets is a lot better for the *family* than it is for her. I cannot bring myself to hire a maid and exploit her, so I exploit my kids instead. When they resist, I badger them–fill them with guilt for not being good members of the family.

My children are lovely people–they give much pleasure–they are still innocent and whole. Anyone can tell you they are "well-adjusted," showing we have a "good" unit going–yet the pressures upon us from this isolated unit often limit them and rend us all apart.

When I was growing up, most of the families that served as my models were not "happy." Many of them were minature Peyton Places with trauma and tragedy permanent residents. Neither I nor they ever considered the possibility that some of their pressures may have emanated from the family institution itself. Again, my religious teachings affected my perceptions. Unhappiness was the human condition. Man was not meant to be content on this earth, only expected to persevere through trials so he could die and begin his real life. As doubts about certain of my religious trainings mounted, I became less willing to defer my happiness. I wanted control over my own destiny–to exercise free will, by making my own decisions and accepting the responsibility for my choices. But not until recently have I questioned the style of family life itself. Before I was content with the myopic determination that *my* family, though existing in similar form to everyone else's, would be *different*–not for me the mistakes of my models. Now I am open to the possibility that for me, at this time, the nuclear family may be exacting too high a price for too little return.

I am not capable of filling every physical, emotional, and intellectual need of even one developing human being, let alone five. Once I thought I was and lived as some superhuman dynamo trying to do so, berating myself with guilt and frustration when I failed. I am fairly relaxed–other mothers speak of my "calmness" and "serenity"– yet I scream at my children inside closed doors, only pride preventing a public display. I overdose them with television. I confuse them with the contradictions in myself–loving and tolerant one day, I am impatient and demanding the next, depending upon my frustrations and physical feelings of the moment.

I oppress my kids so I can survive. No one else sees their scars but I know them well. There isn't a five year old in the world that I can't best with sarcasm. I have done vicious things deliberately because we are all trapped by our way of living. So much for my serenity. And I am stable. The kid with neurotic parents has had it. In our culture, it's a one chance shot for children. You are what your parents can allow you to be.

Almost everyone harbors resentments and hurts from their own parents. Most everyone sometimes resents and hurts their own children and carries great guilt and worry from doing so. The isolated nuclear family can put such intolerable burdens on individuals that it is almost impossible to escape this.

We have evolved such a confining, confined unit that we must adjust to it, not it to us. The time that we should be using to fill the needs of the family members is too often consumed by the pressures of merely maintaining the institution.

***

"Didya ever like somebody a lot and then you got to know him better and you didn't like him so much?"
"Yeh! That's called marriage."

Monogamy is essential to preserve the unit as we know it. One-man, one-woman bound together in a lifetime commitment can certainly have many benefits and beauties, but this too can become warped and oppressive rather than a source of strength and sharing.

Roger and I have an abundant, satisfying relationship. I love him deeply and have never met anyone I would rather live with. Yet I used to oppress him with unrelieved, clinging dependence. For many years, he was totally responsible to fill all my needs, not in a healthy, giving way but in response to a demanding, neurotic dependency. He was my "other half"; without him, I was incomplete. When he wanted to do anything that did not include me, I was perplexed, uncomprehending, and hurt. Why would he *want* to do anything outside of me?

Psychologically, our relationship was a sophisticated boy-girl game, fostered by my teachings of "romantic love." Since we were *one* he should know everything about me, what would please me, and why I was feeling bad. It was against the rules to tell that violets were my favorite flower; he should intuitively know that part of me. When he brought chrysanthemums, my momentary hesitation let him know he had failed me again. It's been so long that it seems unimportant and unreal now, but when I was living it, it was terribly important.

Women have a "need" to be told constantly that everything they do is of value, that they are loved. When Roger didn't notice that I had polished the floor–it he didn't immediately and audibly comment on my contribution to the family–what was the point of doing it? If *he* didn't care . . . This is not an intrinsic need of women. It is a culturally acquired need stemming from our dependence upon one person and our limited role. Every human being needs some feedback upon his performance. Men get this in promotions, salary raises, praise from colleagues. Women only have access to it from their husbands. "But you never *say* you love me."

I created many hurdles for myself because of my refusal to accept responsibility. There was a big tennis tournament in town and a friend gave Roger two tickets. He took the day off and we went. I loved this first introduction to international tennis. The next day, he took off another day to go again, this time his friend using the extra ticket. I was dying to go. It was possible–there were baby-sitters and daily tickets available–but although I hinted broadly, Roger didn't suggest it. I stayed home brooding, until it dawned on me that I was not a child. If I wanted to go, I simply had to arrange my responsibilities and go. I didn't need Roger's permission or his invitation. If he wanted time by himself, I had only to sit in another section.

I got a sitter, drove downtown, and bought a ticket. Roger was amazed and delighted that I would go to so much effort by myself for myself. There was no hurdle here, except a self-imposed one, created by my dependence. I wanted Roger to figure out that I wanted to go and then arrange it- give me permission. When I decided to take charge of myself, it liberated both of us.

Shying away from self-responsibility is common among women. Most of us go directly from our fathers to our husbands. There's more to the endearment, "baby," than meets the ear.

Though Roger does not regard me as a possession and I no longer insist on being one, society still treats me as his. I am Mrs. Roger Burton, my title defines my place. When we married, he retained his sex, but I became a role: "I now pronounce you *man* and *wife*." Insignificant by itself, it defines an attitude that can be oppressive as a whole.

I relate to most people as one-half a couple. We are invited out as a duet: if one is busy, *we* don't go. Rarely would I drop in alone at another couple's house for an evening visit. They would wonder what was wrong. If Roger wants to discuss research with a friend, the friend brings his wife; the women become captive listeners or fill the evening finding a shared interest. Wouldn't it be more sensible for people to arrange their mutual interests exclusive of the spouses?

John calls and asks us to go sailing. I can't go as I am still nursing regularly, but I say that Roger would love to go. He goes and has a splendid day. Two months later, John repeats the invitation. Roger has to teach, so he accepts a raincheck. I do not have to teach–I am finished nursing–there are sitters available–yet it never occurs to Roger or John to ask if I want to go. That would be peculiar, for me to go without my husband.

Why? I am an individual, not an appendage of Roger. Where we go and whom we see should not be dependent upon his schedule. I am an avid sailor, but am never given the option to accept on refuse.

Is there something more? Would it look peculiar because I am a woman and sexual overtones enter? Perhaps that's what looking "loose" means–loose from your owner. Out of control. In our case it only appears to mean that. Roger is also a product of his upbringing; it just never occurred to him that I would want to go without him. I am not entirely convinced.

Months later, Len asks Roger, "I have two tickets to a wine tasting and my wife can't go. Do you want to come?" I tease him, saying, "Why didn't you ask me?" He is abashed (because he *believes* in women's liberation) and then replies embarrassedly, "I just never thought of it–besides my wife would kill me."

The three of us talk about possible reasons for his oversight. The only explanation the men can come up with are sexual implications, i.e., there is a good probability that a relationship between a man and a woman will evolve into a sexual relationship, and our monogamous way of life cannot permit this threat. (That my previous glimpse of this in the sailing episode turns out to be correct is small consolation. I resent being limited to a sexual identity; like any human, am capable of relationships on many different levels.)

If monogamy is so precariously balanced, perhaps it is not so "natural" to human beings after all. There are people of other cultures who live differently. We think of them as savages and fantasize South Sea paradises where people indulge in sexual orgies all day long. Civilized people who must maintain the largest Gross National Product in the world do not have time for such cavortings. But we do not have a corner on morality—these cultures have their own strictly defined moral codes also.

Once, in our missionary zeal, we tried to bend them to our "right" ways of living. For hundreds of years, we persisted in getting them clothed and properly married in church, but we finally recognized the futility of trying to destroy a culture in order to "save" it. We admit now that we know little about human potentialities or the range of human sexuality. We leave most of the primitives alone these days, but we refuse to reassess our own ways of living–continue to impose our strict puritanical notions on ourselves, even though we must practice hypocrisy to do so.

People commonly indulge in extramarital affairs but keep them secret to preserve the sacredness of monogamous beliefs and commitments. Frequent divorce and remarriage show our confusion about monogamy. Are we expected to love only one person in our lives? Or is it only one person at a time?

We are becoming increasingly tolerant of young people's experiments with sexual intercourse. (Research suggests that the "new morality" is not all that new; only the honest admission of it is unique.) We say: "Well, it's better that they get it out of their systems now, rather than marrying and having children and ending up in divorce." Maybe it's in all our systems. Perhaps human beings were meant to be polygamous, bi-sexual, or a whole possibility of things that are too secret and threatening to our present way of life to talk about out loud.

"What will happen to the children?" we wail. Well one thing that will happen is that some people will stop having them, not feeling that reproduction is a necessary route to human fulfillment. Can anyone say that it would not be infinitely better for everyone if childbearing were confined to only those people who truly wanted children? Other people will have progeny and raise them in different settings. With the breaking down of gender stereotypes, it can be realized that a female is not intrinsically more qualified than a male to raise children. Some men are more tender and gentle than some women. The criterion for raising a child should be desire, not sex or a specific mode of living.* Adoption agencies are already recognizing the rationality of this in their newly relaxed regulations on adoptions–many of them now permitting a single person to experience the joys of child-raising.

There are many other possibilities, some of which are in practice now. Children are being raised collectively by many people. This has the potential advantage of the child not being regarded as a personal possession and hindered by his particular parents' vagaries or needs. It can also mean that there are many people present to answer a child's needs. When one adult is tired or irritable, the child can move on to another.

While everyone agrees that a child needs security, no one has proven that many parents necessarily produce an unstable situation. Adverse results are possible, but we *don't know*. We do know that the nuclear family and monogamy are often damaging to a full growth. The other remains an unproven that some people feel worth venturing into.

***

*In my town, there is a collective of twelve lesbians. They are making their sexual commitments to women but they still wished to experience the pleasures of child-rearing. They took an infant to raise, each adult assuming one-twelfth parenthood. Anyone seeing the child at eighteen months cannot doubt her present happiness. She is a smiling, joyful creature, going readily to one and all.

"Well, what's a person to do?"

Though the doomsdayers equate it with the downfall of Rome, the fact remains that today many people are experimenting with different lifestyles and new sexual expressions. Some are choosing communes, collectives, extended familes, group marriages, bi- and homosexuality. There are historical precedents for all of these ways of living. Woven in and out of civilization, they have had both successes and failures. It would be convenient if we could draw exact parallels to prove our prejudices, but no culture has been like us before, blessed with so much affluence, education, and leisure time. Because of our particular twentieth century characteristics, it is likely that our experiments will evolve in forms quite different and unique. Therein lies the risk.

Change of the status quo is always scary, precarious, and full of possible pitfalls–but that is what people are all about. Lower orders must adapt to their environment in order to survive–we are not bound to mere adaptation and reaction, but can bend our surroundings to our desires. Man is the creature that can take chances. People today taking those chances are enduring society's censure and misunderstanding–ignoring the epithets hurled at them, "Unpatriotic!" "Communist!" "Perverts!" "Freaks!" In an ironic way, they are being truly American for they are exercising one of our better myths–that America means that one can have the liberty and tolerance to pursue his own avenue and shape his own destiny.

Some will try new ways only for titillation–others are so repelled by our system that they are eagerly "ripping it off," but every age has had its hedonists and hypocrites. There are many others who are seriously weighing the consequences of their actions, trying honestly to assess and avoid and direct. This is essential, for all new attempts will have to contain a sincere desire to eradicate any lacks that cropped up previously–a woman cooking brown rice in Arizona is not necessarily more liberated than her sister fixing Betty Crocker in Bethesda.*

I'm not an intrepid adverturer–unknowns scare me, too. They can too easily lead to dead ends, or wildernesses, or circle around bringing you back to your point of departure–except that one can never really go back to where she was. Sometimes that's a blessing but not always. Change for change's sake is only appealing to the young and unformed. If it's for growth's sake, then it can be worth the risk and trouble. Many people are not really interested in growing–it's just too hard. Others

---

*Geographical paraphrase of Robin Morgan, "Introduction," *Sisterhood Is Powerful*, p. iii, September, 1970.

will answer their needs in different ways. This is what everyone has to face and answer for herself.

I know that Roger and the children are good things in my life but our present setting is not. I want to join the people who are taking the chances and make a more honest attempt to guide my life into more human and full directions. Roger doesn't feel the need as strongly as I do. He experiences satisfaction daily in his work–I and short exposures still buffer him from many of the frustrations in our life-style. Our children are too young to assign blame or initiate change. So I'm left to bear the brunt of change alone–luckily I'm a woman and genetically endowed for bearing brunts.

I'm not at all certain that I can get hold of our environment, grind it to a stop and start it in a new direction. Certain alternatives are already closed to me. I may chafe at establishment ways, but I'm too old to be a street person. Five kids require me to guide my change within set limitations. Softened by luxury, I'm not willing to share everything. Some privacy is still important, both in space and internally. And the suspicion keeps coming that most communes are not eagerly looking for the lady with five kids.

An extended family seems to meet some of my requirements, living with old and young people, of varying marital statuses, different economic backgrounds. Another possibility is maintaining a single dwelling in the midst of a small community of single dwellings, with shared common areas, duties, and possessions. One inexpensive way to do that would be goedesic domes clustered around one large shared dome.

While Roger hasn't bought a one-way ticket West yet, he has reached the point where we now talk about possible members of our "commune"–we while away pleasant moments thinking of people who have crossed our lives that we could adjust to living with–we haven't yet considered whether they could stand living with us.

I am not bound by the need for permanency. My stability is internal, bolstered by people–my setting is incidental. Perhaps a new life-style will only work for two or three years, or not at all. Five years from now may find me reduced to pitiful pleading, "For God's sake, Roger, let's go home to Bethesda, buy a big brick box, get inside and be ALONE."

Until that happens, I am willing to give up a little privacy for the hope of increased community and a greater sense of self. I'm quite ready to modify my ideas if they infringe on or hurt someone, for I don't reject being a member of a society. No missionary either, I don't bear the one true answer for your unwilling ears. You live your life the way you want to. It's your life. How about a little of the good old yankee freedom and tolerance for mine?

BE HOME WHEN the STREETLIGHTS
COME ON!

CHAPTER 7

BE HOME WHEN
THE STREETLIGHTS GO ON

Roger: "Hi hon, what'd you do today?"
Gabrielle: "Not much. Oh, I signed up for a karate course."
Roger: "You WHAT?"
Gabrielle: "Signed up for a karate course. You know, chop chop. Aie Eiiiiii."
Roger: "Are you out of your nut?"

So there I was on a perfectly fine Tuesday evening–all over the world people were watching TV, going to a movie, or twiddling their thumbs–and I was walking into my first karate lesson. Roger had decided to accompany me, on the rationale that if I were going to learn some crack-brain violence, he'd better learn a few defenses. I wasn't wild about his coming along–it was *my* idea–and I was not eager to expose my puniness to him. But it's a free country, so I didn't mention it.

Nine men gradually wandered in, all giving me various looks of surprise and/or hostility. I just kept flashing brilliant smiles at everyone, while inside the old knots were tightening and the gut was churning–"Aren't there going to be any other *women* in this class?" Nope, I had realized every girl's fantasy–I was going to spend one night a week exclusively in the company of men. Oh well, for once in my life, there'd be no problems of competition–for sure this time, I would be elected "Sweetheart of the Dojo."

The instructor walked over to me. I was relieved to see that he wasn't Oriental–not as a matter of prejudice, but in response to the recurring story that says Orientals resent women butting into a "man's" skill and really make it tough for aspiring Amazons. It may be a myth–actually the Karate code says that all people are equal and should be trained and treated equally–but I wasn't interested in finding out whether my instructor really subscribed to the philosophy.

He stared at me a long time–I flashed him an especially brilliant smile which produced absolutely no response. Eventually my smile drooped and I began to wonder if there were spinach on my teeth. He opened a slit in his granite face and snarled, "Your pants are too tight," and walked scornfully away. I tried vainly to suck my sphincter muscles in to give the illusion of a looser fit.

He snapped us all to attention–told us that we were always to call him "Sir"–and react promptly to his commands. The title was not prompted by grandeur–he *said*, though he distinctly looked a bit Napoleonic to me–but was to be used for reasons of safety and discipline. He put it simply, "When you're an angry dog and want to kill someone, I'll step in and you will react immediately because of instinctual discipline."

I'd like to make it clear right now. I am a really feminine lass and only the accident of being born in northern Michigan prevented me from being a bona-fide Southern belle–but hard work overcame my geographical fate and few people can tell the difference. I've had many aspirations in my life but never once have I aspired to being an "angry dog." "Well, Gabrielle," I said to myself. "You're just going to have to get over a few feminine hang-ups."

Although it fit in with my notions of liberation, I didn't cotton greatly to the idea of being the sole female in the course. I kept slumping and rounding my shoulders (maybe if they don't see that I have breasts . . .) until Sir walked over again and spit out, "Karate is a proud tradition. Stand up STRAIGHT!" (But Sir, if I stand up straight, *they'll* show.) I stood up straight.

We began with a few basic muscular exercises–basic that is, to those who have ever used their muscles. I cracked a few jokes so everyone would know that though a weakling, I was a good sport and a regular fella–but quickly discovered that a karate course is no place for jocularity. I don't know if humorless people gravitate to karate or if karate kills humor, but let me tell you, it is a deadly business in more than one sense.

Old habits of coping die hard. I should have known better but dumbly I tried a little humor again. Peering out at him upside down through my legs, I cracked, "Can we sit down now, Sir? Ha Ha." GLOWER. "Ha Ha," I added again weakly. "Ha?" He decided to straighten me out once and for all. Fixing his eyes on mine–and it was like being face to face with Jack the Ripper–he said, "You have more to lose than any other person in here." In other words, vulnerable female, wipe that vacuous grin off your face. I wiped it.

Sir, who turned out to be John in less dangerous settings, left us in excruciating positions for inordinate periods of time. He *said* that it was a matter of physical discipline but he was smirking all over his mat.

Of course he was right. That's exactly why I had this screwloose idea in the first place. I was gorgeous, charming, and feminine, and I also happened to be lily-livered. Whenever Roger went away on trips, I spent the time indulging in murderous fantasies. I collected all the latest newspaper atrocities and played the central character. It was most inconvenient. I couldn't run the air conditioner because it would prevent me from hearing my killer climb the stairs. The phone was in my room but the children slept down the hall with an open stairway in between us. Now I knew that if it came to the pinch, I was not going to cross that open stairway–where *he* was climbing–and get the kids and race back. Oh no, I would hate myself forever, but I was going to slam my door and wish the best to my children. Now a *mother* can't live with that kind of guilt so I would end up bringing all the children to my room. Have you ever tried sleeping with four little kids in one bed? What sleep wasn't destroyed in listening for noises was demolished by eight feet kicking me in the face.

Finally it seemed rational to learn some form of self-defense, if only for the psychological comfort of it. However, rational ideas are one thing, and thorough feminine conditioning is another. As convinced as I was that it was stupid to keep on living in fear of mayhem–and I was getting so *tired*– I was still a WOMAN and not geared to becoming actively aggressive. I was taught to be passive, to turn the other cheek, to patch up fights–not to win them. I also had the nagging suspicion that though I might learn to give my all in punching some pervert, he would probably turn around and give me his all and I'd end up dead.

As to whether a 90 lb. weakling can really hold her own against a sex-crazed Atlas, a little knowledge of karate quickly dispelled that myth. Sir told us that the majority of all people only utilize about 15% of their body weight in fist-fighting. Proper training can increase this ratio to an 85% usage. Therefore a hundred pound female trained in karate can hit with a force of 85 pounds. Now hopefully she's hitting an untrained 200 lb. clod who's still only using 15% or 30 pounds. If she's taking on someone who also knows karate, she ought to be in a padded cell anyway. Actually, few karate experts indulge in murder and rape as they're too busy attending their thrice-weekly courses.

Sir further pooh-poohed the myth of feminine fragility by cheerfully promising to bring one of his advanced female students to spar with me. "She can hit harder than 90% of males," he said. My response of, "Why bring her?" was ignored.

Even though Sir had reassured me as to my physical potential, I still had a great many psychological barriers to overcome. The whole business was just very embarrassing. First there was that gutteral cry one had to master. Technically called kiyop, it accompanies every move in karate, for both physical and psychological reasons. The most important is that producing the yell correctly expels all the breath out of one's abdomen. If you are punched and it knocks the wind out of you, you have had it. With a breathless abdomen, you can quickly recover and react. It also strengthens the abdominal muscles—a boon for a multipara. Lastly, it's a powerful psychological tactic because it can scare the bejesus out of an attacker.

Valid reasons but the fact remains that it sounds as if one is in the midst of vomiting. For someone who spent years cultivating well-modulated tones, it made me feel like a damned fool. At first I used to fake it, opening my mouth wide in a big grimace but emitting just a tiny sound that I hoped would be swallowed up in the general retching around. At home during the week I practiced it in secret and finally I got pleased enough with the results that it became kind of fun.

The next hurdle to overcome was to learn how to move. I was never big on moving and suddenly I had to *lunge*–to *crouch*–to *hurl*. Once when I reacted to an attack with a little cringing gesture, Sir snapped, "If you're going to do it wrong, at least do it powerfully." (He didn't think much of my "Don't hit me, don't hit me, Mr. Robber," she piteously begged, approach.)

I kept getting the distinct feeling that Sir's reasons for karate were different from mine. He said enthusiastically, "In six weeks you'll be able to break a board in half." While this is a rather pleasant talent and can conjure up simple rewards–"People used to ignore me at parties, now they cluster around to watch me break my board."–it still wasn't my prime goal in life. And for an avowed peacenik, Sir made it a little more sticky by following up his initial remark with, "And remember! A person who can break a board can break a neck.

Meanwhile Roger who was the oldest pupil in the class was clinging desperately to this possible advantage. Sir, who regarded anyone over 25 as having one foot in the grave, obviously thought Rog was some brave old coot and Roger did nothing to dispel his illusion. He spent most of the time talking in a quavery Jonathan Winter voice, saying inane things like, "This karate is pretty hard for an old codger like me. Don't hit me, young fellow. The old bones are brittle." His motto throughout the course remained, TAKE EVERY ADVANTAGE YOU CAN GET. OTHERWISE WE ARE GOING TO END UP KILLED OR MAIMED FOR LIFE.

Occasionally I was accorded a little preferential treatment and when I expressed conflict over deference because of gender, Roger would point out that we were existing in a death-prone setting and I was a simpleton if I made the odds any greater. I must admit to being very happy when Sir was walking around slugging people with a rubber bat and he merely tapped me on the fanny. People were lying on the ground like flies and for once I didn't say, "Equal treatment, please."

Our lives began to be measured out in Tuesday evenings. We would get through one and before we had stopped drawing sighs of relief, bang, Tuesday was back again. Several times we drove round and round and considered throwing in the old chop, but we always ended up going in. It made us wonder about our sanity.

I learned many things. To make a proper fist. Most women clench their fist with their thumb tucked tidily inside which is a sure guarantee of a broken thumb. Fancy that.

That screaming was a bona-fide weapon. Sir never deluded himself that he had a black belt standing there waiting for his Pygmalion touch. He concentrated on getting me to learn a minimum of good quick responses and then to beat it the hell out of there, screaming the whole time.

That I was not powerless and muscular control was not beyond my reach. After a few weeks, I stopped suffering aches in every crevice and savored the blissful feeling that comes from increased control of one's body.

To stop making jokes.

To never consider pitting myself against an assailant holding a gun. Even Old Lightning John himself paid reluctant deference to a gun. Nothing to do but hope, he said. Now if it's a billy club, an iron pipe, or a knife–and his eyes lit up–you've got a chance.

That physical attributes can hinder a person, man or woman. A short person is limited to blinding only short attackers (just in case any of your short friends are so inclined).

I broke Iron John one night. He asked me what I'd do if a guy attacked me. "Kick him in the balls!" came immediately out of my little rosebud lips and he damn near collapsed. From that moment on, I–the little brown wren–was one of the guys as far as he was concerned.

I never learned to deal with the basic bloody concepts of karate. However that was not due to my sex but to ideology. I'm committed to pacifism and non-violence and that's a little tricky to reconcile with the aggressive essence of karate. There were several similarly inclined peaceniks in the class and we used to sheepishly flash furtive peace signals to each other, in between dealing death blows. Every time I would rationalize, "Now look here, Gabrielle, there's nothing noble about getting mugged or raped and you're not going to change the world by submitting." John would spoil my little rose glasses by saying, "There's no muscle course in the world that can build muscles on the Adam's apple. Go for the throat. Rip out the voice box," or "Never completely blind a person. Leave him one eye," or "Tear out the groin and run." He had a million of 'em and they were all violent and repellent. I consoled myself that once I had my body under control, some great spiritual discipline might emerge which would be strong enough to repel force. Like I'd fix someone with deep Jesus eyes and say, "Drop your iron pipe, mister, and come with me and live in peace." Since I seemed a ways from that point, I finally just stopped thinking about the whole contradiction.

In the end, my Walter Mitty fantasy came true. On the last lesson of our introductory course, we paired up for free-sparring, which is a no-holds-barred invitation to maim or be maimed. Roger went first and drew the other "nicest guy" in the course. The two nice guys kept smiling at each other and circling around and then Roger reached out and gave a little chop. Wouldn't you know? It connected to the groin and the other nice guy fell to the floor and writhed for fifteen minutes. I never knew which suffered more crushing–the victim's testicles or Roger's gentle spirit.

Then others went–two at a time while the rest of us stood at the side, silent except for an occasional low whistle. Finally there's just me and the little kid left. Now I *knew* that I was going to end up paired with that little 11 year old, short and fat for his age and barely up to my chin. It would just be another indignity visited upon me, the weaker sex. Well, I've faked plenty of mortifying situations before. I put on my bravado, walked out, nodded to the kid, and said, "Looks like it's us now." John stepped in and said "NO! You go against me tonight." Everyone gasped. Even the bravest nut in the class didn't fantasy sparring with John. Let's face it, John was a KILLER.

I started circling around, doing slow, fancy dancing steps, attempting a little jab here and there, and he said, "Come on now. Really hit me." Well, I don't know what came over me. Suddenly I was no longer Gabrielle, just a housewife with delusions of liberation but chicken guts–I metamorphosed into an angry dog fighting for her life. I moved in–began punching with all my might–all the time emitting the most godawful retching sounds from my throat. I made a mighty connection and John momentarily winced–his face flushed with anger and then–a small proud smile flickered across his face. The rest of the class broke into wild if surprised applause and John reacting to the surprise, wheeled around to them and sneered, "She hits harder than any guy in here." Their faces twitched and the applause dwindled. I bowed to everyone and walked out tall–with my breasts proudly stuck out in plain view.

Now I'd like to tell you that karate has changed my life but that wouldn't be quite true. I do give furtive looks to everyone passing me on the street, a tiny bit disappointed that not one of them has tried to attack me–and I run the air conditioner now whether Roger is home or not, but I can't honestly say that karate is the answer to the women's or even the world's problems. If it taught me anything, it's how very puny a clenched fist is. Seeing even a very powerful man standing there with his little fist stuck out, one is struck by the foolishness of thinking that we can solve violence by a return of violence. In the end the only chance we have is our intellects and our affections but until we're willing to pit them against the clenched fist, karate may hold a partial solution for women.

It may not be "feminine" to yuhhhhh and to chop and to sock. But it's no more feminine to be beaten or ravished or live in fear. The "perfect woman–she submitted unto death" philosophy has got to go.

Presently women are working with a stacked deck and a knowledge of self-defense can at least even up the odds a little. Karate can give one a new perspective on her body as being something more than a sex object or only a vessel of pleasure. Increase psychological confidence by easing debilitating fear. Bring muscular control. Improve posture.

Aid health (if one survives). And just maybe–by demonstrating that women are not intrinsic biological weaklings, subject to the vagaries of brute force, it may help us in the more important battles of the spirit.

CHAPTER 8

PROCEED WITH CAUTION: THE WIFE–THE LIFE–YOU SAVE MAY BE YOUR OWN!

There are all kinds of oppression in the world. Some are quick and crushing and immediately visible. Others are insidious and not noticeable to any except those who are experiencing them. Society has a maddening habit of telling certain people that their oppression is not certified–that their pain is not immediate, overwhelming, or important enough to deal with now. That's a little like a doctor saying, "Well, you've definitely got a low-grade infection going there, but I've decided to work only with cancer patients." Feeling lousy when you came in, you go home feeling lousier that you had the presumption to present your piddling disease.

Most women today are walking around with low-grade infections. Plenty of men are suffering from them, too. Someplace along the line, a lot of men have gotten the idea that the Women's Movement is a movement *against* them. Anyone who really thinks this is either a bona-fide slave-master, paranoiac, or simply hasn't recognized his

own oppression. For the record, the Women's Liberation Movement is a movement against MYTHS–
fables, canards and charades that limit both sexes. It
is a movement for *human* liberation and would be
more aptly titled, "The People's Movement."

"Geez! The *People's* Liberation Movement–that's just
beautiful. But *my* husband says that I can get as liberated as I want between 9 and 5, but not on *his* time."

For all the Hugh Hefners who refuse to see that
"the fate of one sex is inseparable from another,"*
and continue to think of WL as women's whines,
I'd like to point out a few inequities that directly
oppress men.

Kick around alimony for a while. Based on the
notion that women are perpetual financial depen-
dents, it reveals a shattering stereotypical view of
female capacities, but each month who's actually
doling out the old moola? Valid cases can be made
for many women who deserve alimony on the
grounds of "workman's compensation," or "sever-
ance pay," but sometimes it is simply a reward for
failure.** Tell that to a judge.

*Andy Hawley, "A Man's View," *The New Woman,* p. 145.
**In no way do I belie the tragic instances of good
wives who have been blithely turned in for newer models–
or barbarian laws that give no rights or protection to
female spouses. The whole process of separation and
divorce needs radical reassessment.

Toy with enforced conscription. Though talk is big now about doing away with it all, don't bank on it. Politicians have a way of finding "necessary" wars, and wars need fodder. Soldiers are big, brave *men*. The draft ought to be permanently abolished, but if it returns to plague us, I'd like the privilege of having my own draft card to burn.

Try on the "James Bond" concept of masculinity for size. Instead of recognizing it as holding out ridiculously unattainable fantasies of "cock-mastery," a lot of guys end up questioning their "masculinity" when they fail to conquer every passing vagina.

Ever had any gut fears of being a homosexual? Yielded to an honest impulse to embrace-even kiss-a returned male friend? Only the Greeks get away with that.

Cried in public lately? Ever? In front of your wife? Anybody?-since your mother? Any good reason for a male being denied 50% of the emotions on the human spectrum.

Told your co-worker-who may be your best friend-of inadequacies you feel? Don't try it. He'll have your Bigelow in a month.

Thought about that carefully passed down wisdom that a clever female lets a male think he's making the decisions while she runs the show covertly? Really like having an ego that fragile? Or the inherent patronization it reveals?

Resented having all the financial burdens dumped on you, you great big wonderful PROVIDER you?

Secretly wished that your wife weren't *quite* so dependent? Oh, it gives you a little ego trip occasionally, but doesn't it get a little wearing to bear all that responsibility for another adult?

Checked out sexist stereotypes in your home? Of course you don't do the dishes, but who changes the lightbulbs, takes the car to be fixed, mows the lawn? Really dig doing those "masculine" things, or might a little trade-off be nice?

The next time you're scoffing at your wife or girl friend–tenaciously resisting propositions that superficially seem to entail giving up a lot and getting nothing back–look a little closer. The life you save may be your own.

Some men today have already figured out these things and many more. They have formed Men's Liberation groups to further raise their consciousnesses and grope toward more human solutions and ways of living. I'm frankly relieved that they are assuming the responsibility for their lives because it takes the burden off me. I've already misplaced enough energy in one life trying to fix up everyone else's–and I'm up to here with "giver's guilt"–"But he really *needs* me." At the moment, my focus, concern and allegiance is directed toward myself and other women.

Though I do not consider men to be "the enemy," that's a long leap from saying that men have not initiated, perpetuated, and been the main beneficiaries of a society that exploits and oppresses women. Few men have consciously jumped into this role, but birth, tradition, and conditioning have placed and kept them there–and few have done anything about changing it. Males run the institutions in this country, and the institutions thrive by keeping women down. Men hold the power, control the wealth, make the decisions, and start the wars. In all aspects of our society, women have gone along for the ride–resigning themselves to charm, wile and guile to share a little "backsteps" control. In this sense men *are* the enemy, but most are unconscious foes–and in the end, share the victimhood.

Every man in the U.S. is a conscious or unconscious sexist by the mere fact of his accepting the status quo–in exactly the same way that all white people bear degrees of racism by allowing the institutions and conditions that perpetuate it to persist. Well-intentioned, good-hearted men are going to have to face up to this fact and its ramifications; the same way honest white people must come to terms with their racism.

There is no such thing as a "nice guy" who is willing to give his wife freedom. Freedom is not his to give unless he has been her oppressor. The husband who is sharing housework 50-50 has taken a tiny step, but it must reverberate in every other area of his life or become merely a benevolent mockery. If he is still underpaying his secretary, getting kicks from finding "easy lays," or calling a woman "doll," he is deluding himself.

Theoretically women hold the potential of achieving liberation without the active assistance of men. If every secretary in the country laid down her pencil and walked out, pay scales would change soon enough. If all mothers took their children and plopped them in their husbands' offices each morning, childcare centers would be set up immediately. If each wife employed the "Lysistrata" weapon of withholding intercourse until changes came, changes would come. Don't get scared though, for women are not going to utilize this potential power. We have been too brainwashed. Our self-concepts are too weak, and many of us are not sure that we even deserve better than we have. We have been bought off and confused by material possessions and surrogate lives. And we are too dependent and/or scared to challenge the status quo.

In the end, human liberation will only come when the sexes join together to change the institutional conditions that thwart it. The current temporary pulling back of women and men into "women's groups" and "men's groups" is a healthy chance for each sex to straighten out their misconceptions and direct their goals, but at some point, the two will have to join forces and make freedom together.

***

"You may not think much of my suffering
but it's the best one I got."

I'm presently concerned with the masses of
women who are reluctant to join the movement
or even admit its need. Most middle class women
are ignorant of WL, or if informed, are afraid of
its radical objectives. Even those who secretly
agree with many of its goals are reluctant to openly
identify with it because it opens up so many fright-
ening areas. One must come to terms with the
terrifying questions of "Where will I go?" "What
will I do?" "What if I'm wrong?" The quixotic
nature of the whole conflict is further complicated
by the fact that many women simply see no alternatives in their lives. Often they are immobilized by
the real guilt they feel in even entertaining discontent.

The middle class woman has a particular cross
to bear because her suffering is subtle enough
to be trivialized. Enough affluence to buy a surrogate life to sublimate her aches only adds to her
confusion and guilt. But simply because she does
not like to think about her pain and others continue
to scoff at it does not mean that she does not have
it. There are lots of sad, sorry, tiny examples

of suffering around disguised by surfeit, and an abundance of tiny sufferings can end up producing a gigantic unresolved pain.

Consider:

–Women who fritter away their lives day by day, making temporary projects a way of life. "This year I'm going to do the Heart Fund."

–Women who shop as a way of life.
> Play cards incessantly.
> Constantly redecorate their homes.
> Get sick a lot.
> Spend billions annually on clothes and cosmetics to "keep up" and "keep" a man.

–Women who do daytime drinking.
> Pop pills to stay calm.
>> To stay awake.
>> To go to sleep.

–The housewife who daily sleeps each afternoon away. Her decision of whether to also take a morning nap hinges on the flimsy straw of whether the mailman brings "good" mail.

–The young mother who bursts into tears on being told she can't nurse her newborn. Months later, she says, "It was the saddest moment of my life when I found I couldn't breastfeed." A disappointment certainly, but the saddest moment of *one's life*?

–A reading of one's college alumnae newsletter which tells what all your bright, creative schoolmates are presently doing. "I keep interested by playing bridge in two groups and am active in a book club," is a pitiful offering of a former Fullbright scholar. Why should any healthy thirty year old have to do things to "keep interested?"—or another thirty year old, recently married, who is "enjoying a life of leisure." Society would look askance quickly enough at any thirty year old man who casually embraced the same "life of leisure."

–The "Jewish momma" (who can just as well be the "Italian momma" or the "Irish momma") whose overwhelming dominance is a cultural gag. All that creative energy and capability not utilized in any other outlet, having to be released onto the children—bowling them down.

–Elderly women living in an "old folks home," confused and resentful. "I gave my whole life for my children. Why did they put me here?"

–The "good" mothers who do vicious things to their children in secret.

–All the "unexplainable" suicides. "But she had everything to live for."

So many lives and deaths of quiet desperation. Plenty of bread on the table and a second car in the garage paid for by hours of dissociation. Masses of masters of the Scarlett O'Hara survival technique of "thinking about that—tomorrow." Don't presume in your arrogance that this is not real suffering. These women are being written off. In their guts there is often darkness and despair; but when you ask them how they feel, they'll smile quickly and say "Fine." That's only to buy a little more time, more invisibility because they don't know how to retrieve their lives.

I know because I am all these women. I have traveled the same desperate routes and shed uncomprehending tears quietly in the night. It's only by a fluke that I've discovered a little handle to grab onto and get a second chance, but most of my sisters don't even know there's a handle around.

"Oh come now, Gabrielle, you're being melodramatic. You know the real trouble with women is that they sit around and feel sorry for themselves." Self-pity remains a symptom of something terribly wrong–it's not an indictment to hurl scornfully at one.

"You're lucky you're not black or poor, young lady. Quit belly-aching and go back and enjoy your color TV." I am *not* black or poor. I cannot operate through their frame of reference. Because I am middle class and affluent, don't tell me that I must settle for being bought off by possessions.

It makes sense that a ghetto dweller must experience luxuries before he can reject them. But what about those of us who have all that ghetto dwellers yearn for and find that "the good life" is not good for us? Are we supposed to wait for the rest of the world to achieve our standard of living, discover that it has lacks–and then get permission to try something else? Middle class women must get over our guilt about wanting more out of our lives. We are not a great disposable mass.

"I'll admit you've got some valid gripes, but let's take care of the Blacks, the Vietnamese, the Chicanos first."

Let's take care of all of *us* together! Half of all Blacks, Chicanos, and Vietnamese are women who are suffering a double oppression. Then there's me and plenty like me with a single oppressive load that we're tired of carrying. I have forty years left and cannot sacrifice them because you don't know what I'm talking about and resent my even bringing it up.

The Women's Movement is constantly accused of being a middle class woman's frivolous pastime, but it has vast social, political, and psychological implications. It is not a small whimper or a loud whine asking for tiny favors. It is human rights. It is dignity. It is what life should be all about.

Politically and socially, it has intrinsic ties with the endless Asian war and any future wars. As long as we continue to socialize sexist stereotypes into our children–"To be aggressive is masculine." "To refuse to fight is unmanly." "Females should defer to men in 'important' issues."–we will end up with power-seeking males, diffident females, and wars will continue.

Socially it reverberates in the Black Movement. Though many black people scorn it for valid reasons–

–as a natural reaction to multi "once-bitten-twice-shy" experiences;

–as a matter of priority–when you're fighting just to *exist*, spiritual battles have to be postponed;

–in the long-overdue flush of cultural pride–a temporary separatism to find a sense of identity–

the Women's Liberation Movement is going to produce both short-term and long-term gains toward their liberation. Childcare centers, free abortions on demand*, equal pay for equal work, are all immediate necessary advances for everyone, regardless of their source.

Many black women feel that this is the time to get "behind the black brother" and not compete with him, but this is based partially on the acceptance of two misconceptions–the first, the old one again, that the WL Movement is against men–the second, that black women are occupationally better off than black men. Historically, unemployment among adults has been highest for men of minority races, but since 1963 it has been most severe for women of minority races.** Median wages descend in this order: white men are paid

---

*Black Panthers are violently opposed to the demand for free abortions because of the fear of genocide. Their "paranoia" is based on true, tragic instances of sterilization forced on unwilling, unwitting women. Another reason abortion on demand should become an open practice, freed from behind-the-scenes, secret, possibly ulterior motives.

**"Underutilization of Women Workers," U.S. Department of Labor, 1971 (rev.), Chart K, p. 21.

the most, next is *black men*, then white women, and bringing up the tattered rear is the black woman.* She suffers the most discrimination of any in our country.

Long-term gains for non-Caucasians will accrue from a breaking down of sexist conditioning that flows over into our institutions. Much racism thrives on false stereotypes visited upon males. We make sexual identity contingent on tangible attainment-"A 'successful' man makes $20,000 a year." We condition male children to seek success in "besting" and "winning" and often end up with adults who must put others down in order to feel up. With a reordering of values-a concentration on teaching children to be whole and human and derive their satisfactions internally, rather than from external measures-we can remove the need to oppress anybody.

Far from being frivolous, the WL Movement is the most radical of all movements because it is challenging the nuclear family structure, monogamy, sexual expressions, child-rearing practices, the economy, and our ways of thinking. Rather than delaying or detracting from other "causes," it has the most chance of speeding advances in all.

It's fashionable to feel guilty about being middle class. but it's a little stupid. In many areas the

*1969 Handbook on Women Workers, Department of Labor, Table 61, p. 137.

middle class has a record to be proud of—it has often been the impetus for great social awakening, most recently in the civil rights consciousness-raising. Some of our reasons were clouded; and at the outset, we didn't recognize the personal guilt we bore; but still middle class people bore the original vanguard. The anti-war movement was spearheaded by middle class youths. That's a fairly natural evolution—the people who have the education, affluence, and leisure *should* be the ones to perceive injustices and try to initiate remedies.

So I'm not going to beat my breast when you scoff, "Oh, Women's Liberation is just a middle class movement." We are what we are and we're doing what we do because of important, valid reasons. You may scorn my suffering, but it's the best one I've got—and in the end, it's my LIFE, and I've decided it's worth saving. Come along, now or later, as you prefer. You may end up with a new life too.

CHAPTER 9

WHAT A NICE PLACE YOU'VE GOT HERE!
I'M AWFULLY GLAD I CAME

A book is a little like a flirtation or a fight–a lot easier to start than to finish. Chapters are like talking to my Aunt Maud–they have a perverse way of telling tales on their own terms–and you're left at the end with bits and scraps of perfectly brilliant insights, witty lines, and small cogent items–with no place to put them and no ear to hear them. One has the choices of keeping all these delicious things to herself–writing a voluminous, encyclopedic tome that, like the proverbial band, plays on and on and on–or just throwing herself on the reader's charitable willingness to end up with a little smorgasbord. I've chosen the latter route and I hope you'll oblige me by nibbling.

***

I seem to be stuck with my Irish mother's morbid habit of zealously reading obituary pages– and never fail to be apalled by the shabby treatment women get in their final write-ups. Consistently, they are denied any semblance of personal *self* and even in death, must be relegated and

200

resigned to biological accomplishments. Often the obit spins off immediately into their mate's accomplishments. Here is a pathetic little example from today's paper, not unique by any means.

MRS. MASON, WIDOW OF VA. EDITOR–Nancy Galt Mason, 73, died Monday at Staunton Nursing Home, Staunton, Va. Mrs. Mason, a graduate of Hannah More Academy in Reistertown, Md., was the widow of George Carrington Mason. Mr. Mason, who died in 1955, was editor of publications for the Mariners' Museum in Newport News and also served as historiographer for the Episcopal Diocese of Southern Virginia.

Mrs. Mason was the daughter of the late Rev. Alexander Galt. Mr. Galt was rector of St. Timothy's Episcopal Church, Herndon, Va. After his retirement he lived in Falls Church until his death in 1952.

Mrs. Mason is survived by a daughter . . ., two grandchildren . . ., and four sisters . . .

She is also survived by her brother . . .

And I wonder sadly about Mrs. Mason. I know about her long-deceased husband and father, but what did *Nancy* like in life? What did she think? Do? Who was *she*?

***

I never got around to female sexuality. Here I'm in good company because few scientists have ever got around to it either. Sex is with us our whole lives, and it will affect our roles as lovers, wives, and mothers–yet we know next to nothing about *women's* sexuality. All the manuals and books have been written from a male point of view, and women have formed their ideas, practices, and expectations to coincide with that view.

Masters and Johnson have opened up the window a little, but a lot more fresh air is needed. Extensive research remains to be done in all aspects of female sexuality, looking closely at formerly forbidden areas of masturbation, orgasm (clitoral vs. vaginal), lesbianism, and bi-sexuality, to mention just a few provocative blind-spots.*

***

Before I leave sex, never having really gotten to it, I had planned to write a chapter about children and sex. We all know things that we wish our parents had done differently–but most of us ape our parents when it comes to raising our own children. Dr. David Reuban has finally removed the last vestiges of guilt I have over my kids' masturbating, but I did intend to add a few "mother's thoughts" on fingers in the pie and the whole pie for that matter.

***

Why do co-op nursery schools continue to blithely exclude fathers from required participation? This year, my husband went in every fourth week and it remained a constant source of amazement (and pique) to the other mothers. Some

*For a clear, nontechnical explanation of Masters and Johnson's studies, see *Understanding Human Sexual Inadequacy* by Fred Belliveau and Lin Richter.

thought that "a man was more trouble than he was worth" although the children experienced no such ambivalence and gravitated to Roger like the Pied Piper. How come institutions continue to automatically absolve the father from any responsibility for child-raising and people accept it unquestioningly?

***

If epidemiologists saw that there was a profession that did devastating things to many of the people who entered it, their attention and resources would focus on it. Yet this is precisely what research indicates about marriage for women. Married women consistently fare low on testable mental health measures–depression, nervousness, anxiety, etc. Society handles it by telling them to "adjust" and the professional observers ignore it.

***

Women are noted for their depressions. Such megrims used to be accounted for by our hormonal systems. Now psychologists tell us that depression is really unresolved anger. One is angry at some situation or person–sees no hope of changing it or him–and directs the anger inward on oneself. When there is a possibility of resolving the situation, one does it–otherwise, one reacts with depression. Ever wonder why women are noted for their frequent depressions?

***

"When you are young, you always wonder what you'll be doing in a few years. I remember dreaming that in many places. It's a quiet excitement. After I married, I never wondered it again. I *knew* what I'd be doing in five years. The locale might change, but my life would stay the same." One of the most exciting fringe benefits to emerge from the Women's Movement is the return of that heady sense of possibility–an "open" future.

***

VERY PEEVISH PEEVES

People–especially women–who make jokes about Women's Liberation. Clifford Alexander once said that the big difference between WL and Black Liberation is that no one is laughing at blacks anymore.

***

That women are expected to graciously accommodate even while they're being made fun of. Like Queen Victoria, I have reached the point where "We are not amused." It's a little consolation that most jokesters–like Spiro Agnew–will live to regret their short-sighted remarks.

***

Men who dismiss the "radical feminists" with the arrogant comment, "Strident women turn me off." This implies that if someone asks *nicely-politely*, their requests will be considered and that power rests really in the listener's hands. One may bristle at strident presentations but has no right to determine the framework in which an oppressed person expresses her anger.

***

People who call Women's Liberation "Women's Lib." This smirky semantic leads into all kinds of frivolities like "Lib ladies," etc. and visits a faddishness to a deadly serious business. No one would dare to say "Black Lib."

***

People who expect Women Liberationists to slide neatly into pigeonholes. Movement members are sometimes guilty of this also. When I became pregnant for the fifth time, *after* joining the Movement–(Roger misunderstood when I said I wanted a little life of my own)–I had several uncomfortable moments and once was certain they were going to take away my Kate Millett signet ring.

***

Men are always saying, "You don't want to do away with *all* the differences, do you? I'm sure a nice lady like you wants someone to open your doors for you, don't you? *Don't* you?" If it's a choice of paying for an opened door with a closed life, I'm happy to give up the privilege. Actually, I think that whoever gets to the door first ought to open it for the one following. Manners is manners and everyone ought to experience the pleasantries and responsibilities of them.

***

How did the whole business of "entertaining" get started? And get so peculiarly warped? When families lived together and everyone worked and played jointly, the whole notion of Dickensesque celebrations was a rather nice concept. Certainly the idea of greeting the weary traveller with food and drink for the body and refreshment for the spirit still has great merit. But when the traveller's trip consists of a ten minute drive on the freeway and he's repeating the journey once a month, I think he ought to be treated differently. No less warmly, but differently.

Someplace along the line, entertaining has changed from being just a *part* of life to being a *way* of life. With the advent of "leisurely living," a romantic new heroine, the "gracious hostess," emerged. Most of us women quickly glomped onto this new extension. Though it does seem to give housewives a small area for creative expression in an otherwise tedious desert–provides dubious status as "a marvelous hostess" or a "really fabulous cook"–in truth, it has us all aping highly qualified maids (occasionally assisted by a very competent butler, husbands willing). I find it increasingly bizarre that a woman will spend two days making elaborate preparations to "entertain" and "serve" twelve equals–usually be exhausted and preoccupied with mechanics that preclude her entering fully into the enjoyment–have to spend the following day repairing the debris–and then casually toss the whole fretful process off, as "Oh nothing at all, really."

When entertaining is its own purpose and one invites the same people regularly, it's time we approached it on a more egalitarian basis. Or find new friends.

***

I never even got close to problems in the Movement itself and it has plenty. There are many deep clashes among ideologies–the slapdash inefficiency with which most of the Centers are conducted drives many women right up the wall ("If this movement succeeds, it will be *in spite of* itself")– and the glaring lacks we haven't even attempted to cope with, such as the unique problems of the aging woman. Hopefully, with time and fresh blood . . .

***

And to wrap it all up, I'd like to quote my friend, Caroline, who cut to the quick of the quest, many months ago, "I don't want to be the mother of the savior of the world. *I* want to be the savior of the world!" Right on, sister.